With "you are there" realism and total authenticity, **Grey Wolf, Grey Sea** takes the reader aboard
the German U-boat 124 in World War II.

From the day of her commissioning to the day
when she was sunk by a British escort destroyer, this
is a story of daily life in the cramped and complicated
quarters of a submarine, of the crewmen and officers who made U-124 one of the most effective and
famous of all submarines to see action on either
side, and of the excitement and the terror of the
perilous war undersea.

Based on official German records and the vivid
recollections of those who served on U-124 and
survived, **Grey Wolf, Grey Sea** is as close a picture
as we will ever have of the men who fought and died
in the German U-boat service.

Related Reading
from Ballantine Books

When you have finished this book, you will want to read the following titles which provide much valuable information on submarines in World War II:

U-BOAT: THE SECRET MENACE,
   David Mason $1.00
Fascinating, profusely illustrated history of Germany's U-boat fleet, with maps, cutaway drawings and over 100 rare photographs. *A Ballantine Illustrated History*

THE MIDGET RAIDERS, C.E.T. Warren and
   James Benson $.75
Midget submarines, scuba divers, human torpedoes—the whole story of the "underwater commandoes"—with 8 pages of photos. "Hair-raisingly described."
        —New York Times

SUICIDE SUBMARINE! Yutaka Yokota,
   with Joseph D. Harrington $.75
Originally published as "The Kaiten Weapon"—the story of Japan's submarine "Kamikaze" of manned torpedoes. *With 8 pages of rare photos.*

THE SEA WOLVES, Wolfgang Frank $.75
Authentic, complete—the story of German U-boats in action in World War II. "Vivid!"—*New York Times (5th printing)*

U-BOATS AT WAR, Harald Busch $.50
From the easy "kills" of the war's first days to the last desperate patrols, the full story of German submarines in action from 1939 to 1945.

For a complete list, or to order by mail, write to: Dept. CS, Ballantine Books, 36 West 20th St., New York, N.Y. 10003

GREY WOLF, GREY SEA

E. B. GASAWAY

BALLANTINE BOOKS • NEW YORK
An Intext Publisher

*This book is respectfully dedicated to
the men, living and dead, who served
on board the U-124.*

First Printing: June, 1970

Cover art by Ed Valigursky

Printed in the United States of America

BALLANTINE BOOKS, INC.
101 Fifth Avenue, New York, N.Y. 10003

This narrative is based on documents from the United States Navy, United States Coast Guard, the German Navy and published works in the United States, England, and Germany.

Many details were drawn from correspondence and interviews with the men involved, a number of whom I met in Germany several years ago.

The language used in conversations is that used variously in the United States Navy and Merchant Marine, Royal Navy and British Merchant Marine, and German Navy and Merchant Marine.

The U-124 was the third most successful submarine of all the hundreds, Axis and Allied, which fought in World War II. In her short life she sank 49 ships for a total of 226,946 tons.

ACKNOWLEDGEMENTS

Thousands of men and ships took part in the long, complex, and crucial sea war known as the Battle of the Atlantic. This is the story of one fighting submarine and her crew.

The U-124 came to life for me in the personal recollections of men who had served aboard her in times that ranged from terrifying to ridiculous, critical to trivial, nerve-tingling to unbearably dull. All the events, as far as is possible, have been verified, and I have tried to reflect with equal accuracy the thoughts and feelings of the U-124 men. To the best of my knowledge and ability, this book is true.

It is impossible here to name all the individuals who so willingly provided me with the resources necessary for my research, but I must certainly acknowledge a few without whom this book could not have been written.

Wilhelm Schulz took time out from the demands of his own business to help me in every possible way, and the warm hospitality shown me by him and his family made my stay in Germany both productive and pleasant. Also particularly generous with their time and remembrances were Fregattenkapitan Egon Subklew, Rolf Brinker, Karl Rode, Karl Kesselheim, Dr. H. Goder, and the widow of Jochen Mohr. Grossadmiral Karl Dönitz, a.D., and Vizeadmiral Bernard Rogge, a.D., provided information and encouragement, both invaluable. The two British captains, Cdr. Rodney Thomson-Moore, D.S.C., R.N. (ret.) and Lieut. Cdr. Patrick Smythe, D.S.C., R.D., R.N.R. (ret.), now Captain Smythe of the Union Castle Line, were especially helpful in reconstructing the events surrounding the loss of the U-124.

The United States Navy, the British Admiralty, the German Bundesmarine, and the United States Coast Guard all have been kind enough to allow me access to certain documents and records, and I am very grateful, especially to Rear Admiral F. Kent Loomis, U.S.N.

LCDR Arnold Lott, U.S.N., ret., helped me enormously with his criticism and suggestions, both literary and technical. I am also indebted to Roy Bailey and Paul Duval, who went over the manuscript. But for any errors that remain, I am solely responsible.

And, finally, my thanks to the ships M/V MAGDALENE VINNEN and S/S THOMPSON LYKES, along with their crews, who introduced me to the North Atlantic and a sailor's life.

E. Blanchard Gasaway

Hamburg, den 19, Oktober 1964

Men fight—not ships! The destiny of the U-124 described here shows something of the hardness and privation, the courage and the readiness for action, the humanity and fairness of these U-Boat men.

To have been permitted to lead them was for me a particular joy and honor; to have brought them home safe and sound gave me a feeling of thankful grace.

I keep in remembrance those who, in faithful performance of their duty, found their last rest with the boat, Korvettenkapitän Jochen Mohr and his brave crew.

(signed Wilhelm Schulz)
Korvettenkapitän, a.D.

Aumühle, den 28, September 1964

E. Blanchard Gasaway has written this book with an astonishing sensibility of the U-Boat war and the spirit of the U-Boat arm. The events are depicted in a fresh, to the point, and vivid manner—a work very much worth reading!

I wish *Grey Wolf, Grey Sea* much success. I believe that this is in the interest of mutual understanding of the American and German people —which lies so very close to all our hearts.

(signed Dönitz)
Grossadmiral a.D.

Chapter One

IT WAS April 2, 1943. And at last, Commander Rodney Thomson of the Royal Navy reflected, the war news had taken a definitely brighter turn. The German thrust deep into Russia had dissolved into the debacle at Stalingrad; and in North Africa, American and British forces had the Desert Fox Rommel between them. The German army that had seemed so nearly invincible was suffering major setbacks and the land war on all fronts now looked hopeful.

But at sea, he knew, U-boats still prowled, and struck, and killed.

Commander Thomson stared anxiously into the blackness that surrounded his ship, the HMS BLACK SWAN. It was a clear night, but quite dark, and he could not see any of the merchant ships that lumbered along in ragged rows behind him. A feeling of great anxiety, mingled with helplessness, hung over the convoy. The sense of lurking menace was so strong that it was almost a tangible thing.

The two freighters, GOGRA and KATHA, had been sunk since midnight, and the U-boat that had torpedoed them was still somewhere out there. Thomson knew he was waiting in the dark for another chance to attack.

BLACK SWAN swept on in wide zig-zags ahead of the convoy, as the twenty-odd merchantmen behind her struggled to keep station in the dark. Convoy OS 45, now even with the Portuguese coast, had covered roughly a quarter of its long voyage from England to Freetown. As always, the U-boat Command would have known the approximate size and position of the convoy, and would have ordered a scouting line of U-boats to intercept. At least one boat had already found them. Thomson knew that other sleek grey hulls would be silently converging on them as the wolf pack gathered.

Strange how long a man could fight these predators without ever getting a glimpse of one. A U-boat could leave a convoy riddled with sinking and burning ships and not once be actually seen.

Survivors of sunk ships saw them sometimes. Thomson remembered stories about surfaced U-boats with odd emblems painted on their scarred conning towers—a playful dolphin, red devils, a fox's mask, and one with a flower—the edelweiss.

He glanced impatiently at his watch. Not too much longer until dawn.

"Radar reports a stray echo, sir."

Thomson was instantly all attention. "Give me the range and bearing."

The answer came back immediately. The radar operator was Able Seaman D. Hutson, clear-headed and competent. He had plotted the position of the convoy ships, and this contact now was ahead and to starboard. Hutson had recognized it for what it was— a surfaced U-boat.

"Hard starboard!" called Thomson, and braced himself as the sloop heeled over sharply to take the turn.

Her engines hummed with a higher pitch and her hull shuddered with the increased vibrations as BLACK SWAN headed toward the stray echo on a closing bearing. Her sharp prow sliced through the black water which foamed up in white and sparkling bow waves on either side, and her curving wake trailed out behind her.

HMS BLACK SWAN was the first of the "Black Swan" class of anti-submarine sloops, a tough and fast 2,000 tonner, designed specifically for ocean escort duty. She was fitted with the latest in radar gear, eyes that could penetrate the blackest night to see a U-boat riding low on the surface. BLACK SWAN also carried a formidable array of guns, including 6.4" high-angle/low-angle guns in twin mountings. There were two of these forward and one aft, and they had radar incorporated in their fire control. She also carried a number of Oerlicon and Bofors guns, as well as other anti-submarine weapons. She was designed and built for just one purpose—to kill U-boats.

Making her best speed of about 20.5 knots, BLACK SWAN passed close ahead of the starboard wing ship which had loomed up suddenly in the dark. And with every man ready at his post, and every eye straining to penetrate the inky darkness, BLACK SWAN raced toward the ominous echo.

The minutes dragged by. Perhaps the U-boat had already spotted them. Low in the water, she would have a ship in sight long before she was herself seen—unless the ship, like BLACK SWAN, carried radar to see through the dark, and for distances far beyond the sharpest U-boat lookout's capabilities.

Thomson wondered what kind of hand the U-boat skipper was playing. It was highly possible (if not likely), that he had already seen the sloop bearing down on him. Then why had he not sheered off his own course to get out of the way? Was the U-boat, after all, holding the trump card? Thomson frowned. It was not comforting to think that his opposite number's glasses might be trained on him now, and a German fist poised over a torpedo firing button.

Perhaps the U-boat skipper was merely holding his own course expecting the sloop to turn off. He was almost into the convoy, and in the most favorable attacking position possible. Running in front of the convoy, Thomson had been partolling in wide zigzags. If the German did not know he had radar, he would have no reason to suspect that he was not on a leg of his regular search pattern. If this were the case, he would expect the sloop to turn away before reaching the U-boat.

The U-boat must surely have seen him by now. They had to be close, and he was still on the surface. Whatever else her skipper might be, he was cool—and determined. And only BLACK SWAN stood between him and the convoy.

"Radar says he's lost contact, sir."

Thomson nodded briefly at the report. "Very well," he said. The U-boat might be lost in the "clutter," or he might have dived. If the latter were the case, they should soon pick him up on asdic.[1]

"Tell Hutson to keep watching," he said unnecessarily, knowing the radar operator did not have to be told to do his best.

"There!" the lookout above him yelled. "Just off the starboard bow! U-boat, diving!"

Thomson could see the conning tower as it submerged, and he watched as it passed directly in front

---

1. An underwater echo-ranging device, called "sonar" in the U.S.

of the sloop, under water but still visible, some twenty meters ahead.

"Put depth charges on shallow setting!" he shouted.

There was not time to make a planned attack, but the advantage of surprise was on his side. Even if none of the depth charges hit the boat, they might be close enough to shake him up a bit and make it harder for him to evade the next attack.

The water was still boiling with exploding depth charges as BLACK SWAN turned to make another run. The two asdic operators, Lieutenant W. A. Fuller and Able Seaman C. Rushton, reported a contact. Calling out the range and bearing at steady intervals, they guided the sloop precisely to where the U-boat was still desperately plunging downward.

When the explosions had died away, Fuller reported that he had lost contact.

They were now in danger of colliding with the merchant ships and Thomson called for a change of course. The corvette STONECROP was arriving on the scene and she would finish the attack. BLACK SWAN's place was now back in her position at the head of the convoy. They could not afford to leave the front unguarded for long.

Coming in at full speed, the STONECROP, commanded by Captain Patrick Smythe, dropped a pattern of depth charges over the estimated position of the U-boat. When the corvette turned to make another attack, her asdic operator reported that he was unable to make contact.

As STONECROP slowly recrossed the area, now quiet after the violence of exploding depth charges, a shout from a lookout electrified the men on the bridge. "Oil slick ahead!"

The corvette moved slowly through the large and spreading patch of diesel oil, carefully searching for proof of a kill, while her asdic probed in vain for a contact. Only the oil was to be found—the lifeblood of a U-boat, now spreading slowly over the surface of her last battlefield.

At last STONECROP turned and sped away. This battle was over, and now her duties lay with the slow and vulnerable cargo ships which must be protected. Smythe knew other grey wolves were lying in wait for his charges, and he swung his tough little ship back into her station.

Toward the east, the first rosy light was breaking through the darkness. Soon the sun would turn the leaden sea to sparkling blue and green, and pick up rainbows in the dull patch of oil.

Chapter Two

On November 25, 1942, a dark grey U-boat slipped her moorings at a pier assigned to the Second U-Flotilla in Lorient, and turned her prow toward the ocean. A few German navy men stood in the late fall chill to watch as she swung confidently away from the French shore, her own special insignia, the edelweiss, gleaming dully on her conning tower.

This was the U-124, veteran of ten hard war cruises all over the bloody Atlantic. She had come home bearing the scars of savage fights, visible on her grey hull, and invisible on the minds and souls of her men. But along with the scars, some of which would always remain, she had worn the little flags representing ships she had sunk—red for warship, white for freighter, and white with red border for tanker—which told her victories to those watching on the quay when she returned. Now she was going back to the scene of some of her most devastating raids, the western Atlantic. "Grey wolves on a grey sea," a phrase from the U-boat song blaring over the boat's record player, seemed especially appropriate.

A thorough overhauling had put her in first-rate

condition and she ran like new, purring smoothly through the heavy Biscay waves. Caution ruled the day as she passed through these waters, so heavily patrolled by British aircraft and anti-submarine vessels that the area was known as *Toten Allee*—Death Row.

The long shore leave had been as beneficial to her men as it had to the boat, and the intolerable strain of hard months of desperate fighting was gone. Now they felt only the excitement and familiar tightening of nerves that accompanied going back into action, and it was a good feeling.

U-124 was under the command of Kapitänleutnant Jochen Mohr. It was his seventh war cruise on this boat, his fourth as commander. To his crew, there was always a special feeling about going on a war cruise with Mohr. An exceptional leader, he had the subtle intuition and infallibly sure touch they called *"Fingerspitzengefühl."*

His wit and easy-going manner, his boyish charm, and ringing laughter were irresistible to the men who served under him and who felt that he could not make a mistake.

As one young crewman wrote to his mother when she complained about his having to make yet another war cruise, "You must not worry. Always we will sail with our Mohr." *Unser Mohr*—our Mohr.

Besides Mohr, there were other men who had cast their lots and their lives with this boat for one or two or more war cruises. Some were still on board, some had left to tread other decks. U-124 had echoed their footsteps, laughter, jokes, prayers, and curses during the weeks and months when this steel hull was their only shelter from the dangers of the ocean and the enemy, and the shipmates who shared this boat were their only friends.

The always present danger made the closeness of friends more precious and moments of pleasure and triumph sharper and more intensely felt. Their camaraderie was real and strong, but for each of them there were moments of darkness when fear was an overpowering force against which he must struggle alone.

For every man who served on this boat there were ties which he would always feel and each of them left something of his own spirit to remain with the boat always.

With each new patrol there had been changes in personnel, for it was customary to take some of the men who had had battle experience to go on the new boats. The commanders always fought to hang onto their men who had worked up well, and had to be literally forced into giving them up. But with this practice, there was always a sprinkling of veterans in the crews of the new boats, and their replacements learned quickly among shipmates who were already battle-wise.

The custom also served to make the small U-boat service even more closely knit and it seemed that every man knew at least someone on every boat. They went on liberty together in the U-boat base towns along the Bay of Biscay and they listened in on each other's wireless signals at sea. News of the other boats was discussed in wardrooms and messes at sea, in much the same manner that a family might discuss the goings-on of its relatives. They were, in truth, a Band of Brothers.

U-124, unlike most other boats, had inherited most of her original crew as a unit, and their adventures on board the ill-fated U-64 had been told and retold in wardroom and crew's messes until they had become a very part of the U-124 herself.

The story began on December 15, 1939, when the U-64 was turned over to her commander and crew by Deschimag Shipyards in Bremen and taken to the naval base at Kiel for her shakedown cruise in the Baltic. Bad weather soon forced them to break off exercises, and for weeks the boat lay frozen to her pier by the Blücher Bridge in Kiel.

In early March the boat moved to Wilhelmshaven to await orders to the front. The crew now had frequent opportunities to talk to U-boat men returning from war cruises and to learn their experiences and impressions. Some were encouraging to the U-64's untried crew and some were shocking. They began to realize, perhaps for the first time, that what was going on out there in the Atlantic was a cold and relentless war.

While they waited, the crew spent their off-duty hours drinking beer and talking about what lay ahead of them. They were young and keen, and their morale was high. They were proud of their boat and their service, and they were eager to fight.

They began to learn that the easy-going and relaxed atmosphere of a U-boat (as compared with other warships) was not a lack of discipline, but rather an inner discipline, as opposed to strict rules arbitrarily laid down and followed blindly. In the small, tight community of a U-boat, every man aboard was a key man, and on each one depended the safety and success of them all. This huge awareness of his own importance, plus the well-developed sense of humor that made the dangers and discomforts of his life bearable, was the hallmark of the U-boat man.

The boat had been on alert for sea duty for days, so that when her sailing orders finally came, it was almost an anti-climax.

Her commander had been given three sets of orders: first, to escort the raider ORION, under the command of Fregattenkapitän Kurt Weyher, out past the northern coast of Scotland and into the open Atlantic; second, to sink enemy shipping in the Atlantic; and the third were sealed orders, to be opened on receipt of the code word "Hartmuth."

"Both diesels ahead slow," the commander called from the bridge. He was answered by the clang of the engine room telegraph as his order was repeated below.

"Take over the watch," he said to the I.WO,[1] Hein Hirsacker. "When you reach the second buoy, come to half speed and course 330 degrees."

"Aye. At the second buoy, come to half speed and course 330 degrees."

The commander nodded and went below.

"Hey, Bootsmann,"[2] Hirsacker called down to Leo Raudzis on the deck below him. "Is the upper deck clear to dive?"

"As soon as I tighten these gratings, sir."

The boat plowed smoothly through the gentle swells. "See," Hirsacker remarked, "our little steamer lies in the water like a battleship!"

"Upper deck clear to dive, sir," reported Raudzis, climbing onto the bridge.

"Good. Say, Bootsmann, that was a pretty tired farewell back at the pier, wasn't it?"

"I've seen jollier funerals."

They both laughed.

"Well, let's hope we don't get our feet wet," Hirsacker said.

---

1. I.WO (Erster Wachoffizier): First Watch Officer, executive officer.
2. Bootsmann: Boatswain, petty officer.

"Second buoy ... ten degrees to starboard," the lookout interrupted.

"Good. Both engines half ahead. Come to course 330 degrees."

"Both engines half ahead. Come to course 330 degrees," a voice below him echoed, followed by the shrill engine room telegraph and the acknowledgement that his orders had been carried out.

Then he called the commander on the speaking tube. "Bridge here. First watch officer reporting the watch set and ready for action. Second buoy on starboard. Course 330 degrees. Both engines half."

"Thank you," the commander replied. Then he called to Kurt Oehring in the radio room across from his own cabin. "Hi, any signals for us?"

"No, Herr Kaleu," Oehring answered, using the abbreviation for his commander's rank, Kapitänleutnant.

"Very well. See if you can get us some music."

U-64 was under the command of Kapitänleutnant Wilhelm Georg Schulz, a gifted officer who possessed a wealth of seagoing experience, in addition to the most thorough training the German Kriegsmarine could provide. He had first gone to sea at the age of 17 as an ordinary seaman on a small merchant ship powered by sails alone, lacking auxiliary engines and even wireless. His first voyage took him to Australia and the South Seas by way of the stormy Cape Horn, and had lasted a year and a half. He had seen most of the world and earned his master's papers by the time he came to "Uncle Erich's[1] Steamer Company" from a berth as fourth officer on the luxury ship OCEANA of the Hamburg-Amerika Line.

For generations, the men in his family had been army officers. His father had been an artillery major,

---

1. Erich Raeder, commander-in-chief of the Kriegsmarine.

and his brother Heinrich was a General Staff officer. Serving his country came naturally and easily to him, and so did the decisions and responsibilities of command. To outsiders, he often appeared cool and somewhat unapproachable, an officer cast in the rigid mold of Prussian discipline and bound by the highest ideals and standards of the German officer class.

His crew, however, had soon discovered for themselves that he was a man who understood them completely and who was genuinely concerned about them. Every sailor on board knew with certainty that he could go to his commander at any time with his problems, personal or otherwise, and knowing this gave them confidence. He set high standards for himself and for them, and his boat was tight and well-run. He seemed rather like a father to the 19 and 20 year olds, whose first awe of him had quickly turned to open admiration and absolute trust. They nicknamed him "Willem," a fact they discreetly kept from him.

On April 9, U-64 and her charge, ORION, which was disguised as an ordinary freighter, were still in the North Sea, in the vicinity of Edinburgh, when a wireless message arrived from U-boat headquarters addressed to U-Schulz. It contained the single word: "Hartmuth."

Schulz opened his sealed orders, and then called his crew together to tell them that their destination was Norway, to protect the fjords at Narvik. The invasion of Norway had begun.

Bidding farewell and good hunting to the ORION, U-64 turned her bow toward Norway and the icy waters that would be her grave.

After a couple of days hard steaming, U-64 had entered West-Fjord on the way to Narvik. The German ships were already in position and had landed their troops. The city of Narvik was in German hands. But British battleships, cruisers, and destroyers had arrived also, and they now occupied the outer positions, bottling up the German ships in the fjords. U-64 crept cautiously into West-Fjord in daylight and on the surface.

"Ship bearing 25 degrees," a lookout called.

The commander briefly searched the position. "Ah, there she is. Destroyer. We'd better head for the cellar. Now what's she steering?" he asked himself. "Eighty-five degrees. Fine." Then he called, "Clear the bridge! Make ready to dive!"

A shout came from below him in the conning tower as Willi Klein echoed, "Make ready to dive!"

The order was repeated in the control room as the bridge watch skidded down the steel ladder from the bridge. The commander followed, slamming and dogging down the hatch above him. "Hatch is closed! Dive!" he called.

"Dive!" the L.I.[1] repeated, the word losing itself in the rush of water pouring into the diving tanks as well-trained hands flew swiftly and surely among the maze of valves and levers. The throbbing diesels were shut off and replaced by the two electric motors that drove the boat under.

The chief engineering officer was an enormous, easy-going Bavarian, Oberleutnant zur See (Ing.) Steinmetz. A popular man, he was a walking example of "Gemütlichkeit," the special warmth, gaiety, and friendliness his home is famous for.

"Come to periscope depth," Schulz said quietly, shouts no longer needed above the softer hum of the electric motors. "Bring her to 10 degrees, Klein."

---

1. L.I. (Leitende Ingenieur): Chief engineering officer.

"Steering 10 degrees."

"Boat is at 14 meters. Periscope clear," Steinmetz reported.

"Both ahead slow," Schulz ordered, and was answered by the clang of the engine room telegraph.

"Man, cut out that racket!" he snapped as he pressed his eyes to the periscope.

The boat began her approach, Schulz taking quick and wary looks through the periscope at intervals. Finally he established her identity. "She's British. Make ready tubes one and two."

Word flashed through the boat, and the crew exchanged confident grins. Their first target—their first *victim*, rather—and a destroyer at that!

"Tubes one and two ready!"

Schulz squinted through the scope. "L.I., can't you hold the boat steadier?"

"It's damned difficult, Herr Kaleu," Steinmetz replied. "The sea way is too strong. It rolls her under." He spoke brief orders to the planesmen sitting in front of him, his eyes fixed on the array of gauges and dials over their heads.

"Both dead slow," the commander said.

"I can't hold the boat dead slow," Steinmetz told him.

"Try," Schulz replied unperturbed. Then he cried out excitedly, "Damn! If she stays on her course, she'll come right in front of our tubes! Enemy speed 20 knots, course 115 degrees, own course zero degrees, distance . . . 800 . . . 700 . . . 500 . . . tubes one and two . . ."

There was a quick breathless silence in the boat as they waited for the "Torpedo . . . *los!*" that would fire the torpedo.

"L.I., take her down!" the commander shouted.

"Both engines ahead full! Hard port! Close outer doors!"

The crew knew they had been seen, and knew further that if they hoped to escape, they must get deep and get there fast. The relief they felt as the boat began plunging downward was short-lived, however, for as suddenly as she had started down, she twisted violently and broached the surface.

Steinmetz checked his instruments frantically, and found the answer right before him. When the order was given to submerge, someone had blown the port diving tank instead of flooding it. It took the L.I. only seconds to flood it, and U-64 had obediently settled down to 80 meters by the time the destroyer roared overhead.

The depth charges were wide, but the boat quivered with shock waves and they sounded like doom to those who were hearing them for the first time.

Willi Klein turned around wide-eyed. "Did you hear that, Sherry?" he whispered, using the familiar nickname that had been hung on Karl Kesselheim by a harried drill instructor who got tired of trying to distinguish among three Karls in one squad.

"Hear what?" Kesselheim asked innocently.

"The bombs!"

"No."

"Ass."

U-64 soon lost the destroyer, and her elated crew congratulated themselves. They had shaken off their first destroyer and had done it easily, even in these narrow fjord waters. The famous British asdic that was supposed to end submarine warfare had not quite lived up to its claims, they thought smugly.

Their commander was neither elated nor smug. He had almost lost his boat, simply because of a stupid mistake on the part of one of his own crew and he was furious.

There was no time to dwell on past mistakes, but his young, green crew would have to learn and learn fast. They were running on the surface in British-held waters, and their batteries were perilously low. He got off a hurried report to headquarters: "Strong destroyer guard stands before the fjord. Narvik threatens to be a trap."

At the end of West-Fjord, they could see two cruisers with a screen of three destroyers. There was no doubt this time that they were British.

"How much juice left in the batteries, L.I.?" Schulz asked.

"They're pretty low, sir," was the answer. "Enough to attack, not much to escape on."

The commander hesitated. Escape was obviously impossible on the surface, and his almost depleted batteries would not hold out for an underwater chase. Schulz knew that the aggressiveness Dönitz had pounded into them did not in any way include suicide. The risk was overwhelming, but two enemy cruisers lying dead in the water was too tempting a target to pass up. Besides, he reasoned, if his attack were successful, the destroyers should be too busy picking up survivors to give chase.

He took his boat to periscope depth, and set up the firing data as he moved into position.

"Fire one and two," he ordered. Then, "Down periscope!" as he began to count off seconds on the running time.

The silence in the conning tower was suddenly broken by two loud explosions. The officers looked at each other questioningly. The torpedoes could not have run more than half the distance to the target.

Schulz jerked up the scope for a hasty look. Both

torpedoes had exploded prematurely. As he would learn later, this torpedo failure was one which would plague every U-boat in the Norwegian campaign. The only thing his torpedoes had accomplished was to announce his presence to the destroyers, and they were already charging out to find him.

"Take her down!" Schulz yelled. "Both ahead full!"

U-64 dived deep, and the destroyers were unable to locate her as she moved away on creeping speed. The depth charges they dropped were not close.

Schulz turned to the chief engineer. "The batteries?"

Steinmetz shook his head. "They're about gone."

Schulz glanced at the officers and men around him. Their position was hopeless—pursued by two enemy destroyers and their batteries were used up. To surface was suicide.

"L.I.," he beckoned to Steinmetz, "you, Raudzis, and Wagner set the scuttling charges. We'll have to come up soon. The men will go over the side, but the Tommies can't have my boat."

Kesselheim stopped Raudzis as he trudged despondently by. "Wait, Bootsmann. What's going on?"

"We're setting the scuttling charges. The batteries are used up."

"What about us?"

"Make ready to die."

Kesselheim ran back to his locker and returned with a toothbrush in his hand. Willi Klein looked at him in astonishment.

"Have you lost your mind?" he demanded. "You're going to brush your teeth at a time like this?"

"They might not have one for me in the prison camp."

Rudi Dimmlich glanced over at them. "Do you think they'll fish us out of the water?"

"Oh, sure," Kesselheim replied confidently. "They're sailors, same as us. What sailor is going to watch another one drown if he can help it?"

"That's *if* we manage to get through the machine gun fire they'll be spraying us with when we surface!" Willi added grimly.

"*Bootsmann*," the commander's clear voice cut through the confused murmur, "are the scuttling charges set?"

"They're set."

Schulz took a deep breath. "Very well. Bring her up to periscope depth, L.I."

The boat nosed gently up as the electric motors drove her toward the surface.

"Periscope depth, Herr Kaleu."

Schulz scanned the horizon around them, then turned, a broad grin on his face. "Take her down!" he ordered crisply. "Hard starboard. Come to 140 degrees. We just might make it yet!"

The destroyers were still plainly visible, still searching, and he could not surface without being seen. But he had seen something else in that brief look around—something that might give him a chance to save his boat after all.

He knew these waters well from many a carefree day on board the beautiful and luxurious OCEANA. Now a lighthouse which he remembered from these cruises had pinpointed his position precisely. They were closer to Narvik than he had realized, and he knew now if he could get around the curve ahead of them, they would be safe.

"Steinmetz!" Schulz called. "Come here! How much juice left?" he asked.

"Not much," the L.I. shrugged.

"How much, man?" persisted Schulz impatiently. "How much longer can we stay under?"

"Can't tell, Herr Kaleu," answered Steinmetz. "They're almost dry. Maybe half an hour. Maybe less." He shrugged again. "I just don't know."

"Very well," Schulz replied. "We'll stay on creeping speed. If they'll get us around that bend, we're safe."

If the anxiety had frayed the commander's nerves, his men could not tell it. He now stood in the control room, calm and self-controlled, while he fought for their survival with every ounce of skill, toughness, and tenacity he possessed.

This was Schulz's first command of one of the larger Type VII C boats, the ocean-going U-boats designed to fight in the Atlantic convoy lanes. Before taking over the U-64, he had been commander of a U-10, a small (250 ton) coastal boat, and had made two war cruises around the Orkney Islands. She was too small to carry fuel and supplies for an extended operation, and also lacked the space for the torpedoes which would make such a cruise worthwhile. She was better suited for training than operational purposes, but Germany was in desperately short supply of boats.

But U-64—now that was another matter. Here was a boat a man could fight with! Wonderfully maneuverable, she handled like a speed boat, needing only seconds to dive, surface, or turn. She could leave base crammed to the brim with fuel, supplies, and torpedoes, and could fight anywhere in the North Atlantic. She was a fine craft and her commander was determined not to give her up as long as he had a single card left to play.

"Come to periscope depth," his quiet order broke the silence.

He stooped to catch the handles and straightened up with it as the periscope rose in the housing. He watched the dark water grow lighter as they neared the surface until the periscope broke through the foamy green wave tops, and he quickly scanned the sky for planes. Then he took a hurried sweep around the horizon. Nothing. The two destroyers were still in sight, but far behind them. And they had reached the bend in the fjord.

"Hard starboard!" Schulz called to the helmsman, and turned with a triumphant grin.

It was only a matter of minutes until the destroyers were lost to sight, and he gave the order to surface. As U-64 reached the surface and the diesels came to life with a shuddering roar, Schulz yelled down from the bridge, "Hey, L.I.! Well done!"

The engineer's face appeared below him in the control room. "Thanks, Herr Kaleu'nt," he shouted back. "But we run on the surface now. There's not enough juice in the batteries to make one more rev on the screws!"

"Don't need it now, L.I.," laughed Schulz. "The next destroyers we meet will be ours."

He turned back to the waters in front of them. The smile suddenly froze on his lips and his eyes narrowed.

"Herr Kaleu'nt," the lookout's alarmed voice began.

"Yes, I see it," Schulz interrupted. "It has to be German."

They watched anxiously as the other submarine approached on the surface. But it took only a minute to exchange recognition signals, and soon they were alongside each other.

Schulz hailed Viktor Schütze, skipper of the U-25, and asked about conditions ahead. Schütze told him there were no enemy units between them and Narvik and offered to act as a rear guard when he learned that U-64 was unable to dive. They reached Narvik safely about noon.

That afternoon, the commander was on board a

destroyer to receive his new orders when an air raid alarm brought him to his feet in a frantic dash to get back to his boat. But when he reached the destroyer deck it was too late. He could only stand and watch helplessly while the bombs rained around his U-64 as she lay vulnerable and unprotected at the pier.

When the smoke had cleared, he could not see any damage to the boat, but he could not breathe easily until he got back to make sure she was safe.

U-64 was soon made ready for sea, and within only a few hours after her arrival, had cast off and headed toward the open sea. Her orders were to sink all British ships coming in.

Schulz turned his boat into the adjoining Herjangsfjord, which would put him in a position to observe and attack any ships coming through Ofotfjord on the way to Narvik. It was April 13.

The boat had almost reached the position her commander had chosen for her to submerge and lie in wait for enemy ships, when without warning, a small pontoon plane from the British battleship WARSPITE swooped down out of the sun. The mountains ringing the narrow fjord had concealed the plane until it was almost upon them.

"Make ready to dive! Hard port!" yelled Schulz. Then, "Man the deck gun!"

There was no time to dive before the plane's first run, but they could hit the cellar the instant it passed overhead, and would be reasonably deep by the time it could turn and make another pass. The 2 cm. deck gun offered their only chance against this first attack.

Karlchen Wenzel managed to get off a few erratic rounds with the deck ack-ack, but they missed the plane that roared over their heads and dropped a bomb squarely on the bow. The boat leaped in the air and shuddered like a wounded animal, throwing some of the men into the guns and periscope, and some overboard.

As soon as the noise had died away, damage reports came to the bridge from below. The men in the forward compartment where the bomb had hit were dead, and the boat was taking water rapidly.

"Everybody overboard!" Schulz shouted to the men topside. Then he yelled down the open hatch, "Get the men out! Hurry!"

"Hurry up!" came Steinmetz's voice from below. "Get a move on if you don't want to get your feet wet!"

As the deck shifted beneath his feet, Schulz realized she was going down too fast for the men to get out. But he also knew the water under them was only about 35 meters deep, and that the crew could come out when she settled on the bottom. They had practiced for just such a need, under the careful supervision of an instructor who had once held the world's deep sea diving record. Schulz had no doubt that they would reach the surface safely.

"Here, Piepenhagen," he said, "go back in and tell the men to put on their escape lungs and when the boat reaches the bottom to come out the way we practiced."

Bootsmannsmaat[1] Arthur Piepenhagen quickly climbed back into the conning tower, and Schulz slammed the hatch behind him. As he did, the boat slid from beneath his feet and he was left swimming in the freezing fjord water.

He struck out in the direction of shore. Ahead of him he could hear the other men splashing along, then he heard shouts from the direction of land as boats were launched to come to their rescue. He swam

---

1. Bootsmannsmaat: boatsman's mate.

on, but each stroke was weaker than the last, and he could feel his water-soaked clothes dragging him down. The numbing cold and exhaustion were taking their toll, and he knew he could not stay afloat until the boats reached him.

From nearby one of his men shouted, "Hallo, I've found a barrel! Does anybody need help?"

"Over here!" Schulz gasped. "Come to me! I can't swim any more!"

"Hang on! I'm coming!"

A few seconds later the sailor reached him, pushing the empty oil drum in front of him. Schulz grabbed hold and the two paddled slowly toward shore. He had no idea where the thing had come from, perhaps from one of the ships that had been sunk during the fighting in the fjords. But he knew it had saved his life.

German voices hailed them, and they looked up as one of the small boats drew alongside them and willing hands pulled them aboard. The men in the boat told him they had seen the plane bomb the U-boat, and had set out to pick them up when she sank.

Schulz pulled the blanket closer around him as he sat huddled in the bottom of the boat and stared absent-mindedly at the insignia his rescuers wore. It was the little mountain flower, the edelweiss, emblem of the German Alpine troops. These elite mountain soldiers had taken part in the invasion of Norway, and were now encamped along the bank of the fjord. They were, Schulz reflected wryly, the last people he'd expect to rescue a shipwrecked sailor.

As soon as they reached the shore, the soldiers took them inside and stripped off their wet clothes. They rubbed their half-frozen bodies dry and wrapped them in blankets. Then they gave them red wine to drink, but it would be hours before the U-boat men would stop shivering.

Schulz had hastily counted heads among his crew and saw that thirteen, including himself, had been rescued. These were safe. And now his concern rested with the others, the ones who would soon be swimming in the fjord.

"Send for your commander," he ordered one of the soldiers. "I must see him at once."

The colonel in command of the Alpine troops listened attentively as the shaking and shocked U-boat commander told him to send his men back in the boats to get the rest of his crew.

"Yes, Herr Schulz," he murmured sympathetically as he filled his glass with wine. "I know how you feel, but we have rescued all your survivors. There is no one left out there."

"But you don't understand, Herr Oberst," persisted Schulz, feeling somewhat at a disadvantage, dressed as he was in nothing but his own skin and an army blanket, and trembling like a leaf. "My men will be there in twenty minutes."

"Yes, yes," the colonel said kindly, "just drink your wine. Everything will be all right."

"Nothing will be all right if you leave my men out there to freeze or drown," shouted Schulz.

"Please, Herr Schulz, you must calm yourself," the colonel pleaded. "Drink this," he said, feeding him another glass of wine.

"Herr Oberst, for God's sake listen to me!" Schulz howled, almost in tears from shock and frustration. "I tell you the rest of my men will come up out of the boat, and somebody must be there to rescue them or they will die!"

The colonel sighed. This poor U-boat commander was obviously delirious and on the verge of hysterics, and apparently was not going to thaw out, get drunk, go to sleep, or anything else until he got over this mad delusion that his lost crew would somehow magically reappear.

"Leutnant!" he called. "Get some men in the boats to watch for any more of the U-boat crew that may come up."

"Sir, we have rescued all of them," the lieutenant told him.

"Go anyway."

The lieutenant's face was puzzled, but he kept his thoughts to himself, saluted, and walked out.

The colonel turned back to Schulz. "Does that make you feel better, Herr Schulz?"

Schulz smiled weakly. "Yes, Herr Oberst. Thank you very much."

"Then you'd better have a little more wine and try to get some sleep, Commander."

"I'll wait until the rest of my men get here," Schulz replied. "I'll sleep better when I know they're safe."

The colonel shrugged, and looked at the U-boat commander pityingly. He had been through a difficult ordeal, and the strain had left its mark on both his body and his nerves. He still trembled from the cold that had numbed him to his bones, and he could not seem to grasp the fact that only this handful of survivors remained from his lost U-boat. Well, these U-boat sailors were strong men, picked men, like his own mountain troops. It would not take them long to recover, and in the meantime, it would not hurt to humor their bewildered and unstrung commander.

The attack by the plane had caused the utmost confusion inside the boat. At 1200, Karl Kesselheim had gone on watch in the radio room. He had not already eaten because the cook, Adolph Schäfer, was late with the pork chops, a fact to which many of the crew would owe their lives. Had dinner been served on time, half the men would have been in the forward compartment where the bomb landed.

Kesselheim had just tuned in the war news report when he heard the commander's urgent order, "Stand by to dive," and to man the deck gun. Next he heard the barking of the 2 cm. flak gun. He tried to make out from the men in the control room what was happening, but they were as confused as he.

Then two explosions shook the boat, and the unexcited voice of the radio commentator announced the time. It was 1313 hours.

The bow trembled with the inrushing water, and then for a few seconds the whole boat was deathly quiet. Kesselheim had decided that the damage was not as great as he had first thought, when he heard the commander's voice ordering everyone overboard.

The boat was already secured for diving, which meant that the water-tight hatches were dogged shut. The boat was now cut into several separate compartments, so that only the forward compartment was flooded, but it was enough to drag the boat down. Men raced frantically to the ladder in the conning tower, guided by the old rule of "every man for himself." They were not melodramatic heroes to stand bravely smiling while meeting their doom, but simple sailors who had wives and sweethearts and a desperate desire to live.

Kesselheim had just reached the conning tower when the hatch above him slammed shut and the boat began to sink. His hands gripped the cold steel of the ladder, and the terror he had felt was suddenly replaced by an overwhelming sadness that he was really going to die. It seemed such a pity, and he was sorry that he would not at least live to see his 21st birthday. Suddenly a soft bump broke into his thoughts as the boat gently settled on the bottom. To his surprise, they now lay still at a depth of only 35 meters.

Directly under him, his buddy and fellow radio man Willi Buhl muttered, "We've got to open up the hatch. Give me a hand, will you?"

The two climbed up and shoved on the hatch together. They struggled diligently until the foolishness of it suddenly dawned on Kesselheim.

"We're idiots, Willi," he said. "How do you think two men can push against the sea pressure outside?"

Suddenly Buhl began to shout wildly, "Get some explosives! We've got to blast it open!"

The others tried to quiet him, but he kept screaming until the burly Hänschen Fröhlich shoved a fist under his nose and calmly informed him that he was going to break his neck if he did not shut up. The unmistakable seriousness of Hänschen's threat brought him to his senses, and he smiled faintly and moved his hand in an awkward apologetic gesture.

Piepenhagen had relayed the commander's instructions and begun the necessary procedures for escape. The men had managed to locate a few life jackets and escape lungs, but since most were in the flooded forward compartment, there were not enough to go around. Fortunately, the water was not deep enough to make either essential.

There was nothing to be done for the moment but to wait, and for each man to hold his nerves in check against the paralyzing fear that ran through the boat like an electric current.

Kesselheim left the crowded conning tower and went below. The water was rising steadily as he, now alone in the control room, sat on the chart table musing over his fate. It occurred to him that there might be someone in the diesel engine room, so he sloshed over and banged on the door with his fist and shouted.

After a time, he heard a voice through the speaking tube. It was Maschinistmaat[1] Walbröl. He asked how high the water was in the control room and if the door could be opened without flooding the engine room. When Kesselheim assured him it could, the heavy steel door was shoved open. Inside were about 20 men.

Although the after part of the boat was still dry, it would be necessary to flood it. This was a requisite before they could escape, and normally, it was a fairly simple procedure which required no more than a quarter of an hour. It was necessary to have enough water in the boat to flood the escape cylinder and equalize the pressure inside the cylinder to the water outside the boat so the hatch could be opened. This would still leave plenty of breathing space for the crew.

However, in this case, the boat was lying at an angle of about 45 degrees, which caused some problems. It was extremely difficult to move about on the boat, and it was necessary to have many extra tons of water in the boat in order to flood the escape cylinder. The incoming water soon reached the batteries, and they were left in darkness, except for the light of one emergency lamp.

The water rose and rose. Some of the men climbed on the port diesel to get out of it. Thus they stood or sat and talked, mostly of unimportant things, while they waited, and the numbing cold water rose almost to their necks.

One of the torpedo mixers, Hannes Wiegand, always a gay and happy boy, suddenly announced re-

---

1. Maschinistmaat: Machinist's mate.

gretfully, "If I'd known this was going to happen, I wouldn't have paid my bill at the canteen."

The two engine room petty officers beside him were quietly discussing their life expectancy. Fred Humke asked Phillip Luft, "Do you think we'll get out of it?"

"Sure we will," Luft said firmly. "You'll see your wife and children again."

"Do you really think so?"

"Absolutely!"

Behind them a voice was dispiritedly droning, "We'll never get out. We'll never get out."

The chant went on and on, until Phillip Luft turned around and said coldly, "Now if you don't mind, please play the other side of that record."

"We'll never get . . ."

"I said shut up!"

One of the men began to pray softly, "Holy Mary, Mother of God . . . stay by me . . ."

Willi Klein interrupted him, half-joking, half in earnest, "Just a minute, friend. We're here too, you know."

"God, if it just weren't so cold!" a trembling voice murmured through chattering teeth.

A man collapsed silently and slid under the water. Hans Wiegand and Phillip Luft quickly pulled him up again, but he was dead, apparently from heart failure. He was Karl Reichenthal, one of the diesel machinists, a well-liked Bavarian, nicknamed Kraxel.

It was growing more and more difficult to breathe. Kesselheim's thoughts were drawn inevitably to Reichenthal—at least it was over for him. Kesselheim almost envied him and wished he could die so easily, so quickly. How long did it take a man to drown? Five minutes? Surely not so long—surely he would be conscious no more than three.

At last the cylinder was flooded, and it was time to try it now if they were to get out at all. Rudi Dimmlich, a machinist, went first. They waited two or three minutes. Either Dimmlich was out or he had drowned in the cylinder.

Kesselheim put on the life jacket Dimmlich had given him, and Luft caught him by the arm. "Go ahead, Sherry. You're next."

Kesselheim climbed into the cylinder. He had been afraid he would not be able to hold his breath long enough to reach the surface, or that he would be trapped in the cylinder and drowned, but as he started up, the immense relief at getting out overrode all his fears. He opened his eyes and watched as the boat disappeared below him. He seemed to be rising at about the speed of an elevator, and soon he could see the rays of sunshine through the waves.

At last he reached the surface. The snow-covered mountains around him were indescribably beautiful, and he was so happy to be alive and out of the doomed boat that he did not even feel the cold any more. He could see a boat about 50 meters away with three men in it. One of them was Rudi Dimmlich. At the same time he felt himself grasped by the back of the neck as two soldiers behind him reached out and pulled him into their boat.

U-boat men were bobbing to the surface like corks, and soon they were all fished out. When Kesselheim's boat reached the shore, he could see Hänschen Fröhlich lying in the next boat, unconscious and bleeding from the mouth. With him were the men Kesselheim had seen in the conning tower.

When he had climbed down, they had closed the hatch behind him and flooded the conning tower through the speaking tube to the bridge. Six of the eight men inside had then gone out through the bridge hatch.

Fröhlich was able to remember only parts of the experience. The pitch blackness inside the conning tower had forced them to feel their way, and the angle at which the boat was lying had helped to further disorient them. Fröhlich blacked out and did not remember leaving the boat. He was picked up unconscious on the surface. Kurt Oehring and Willi Buhl did not get out, no one knew why. Three months later, Buhl's body was found floating in the fjord. The boat had turned him loose.

By now, Kesselheim was hurting from head to toe. His legs were almost paralyzed, but he pulled away from the soldiers who tried to help him, determined to get ashore under his own power. The doctor who was waiting for them patted him sympathetically on the shoulder and said, "You're brave fellows." Kesselheim promptly collapsed in a heap.

The survivors were temporarily put in private homes along the shore to thaw out and recover. So Kesselheim, in the new warm underwear he was given, crawled into bed with Maschinist Franz Grenz. They lay shivering, their teeth chattering like castanets, and laughing with the sheer pleasure of being still alive, while the woman of the house and her daughters washed out their burning eyes.

A little while later they joined several of their shipmates in the living room. While they were trying to estimate how many of them had gotten off the boat, one of the sailors looking out the window suddenly called, "Hey fellows, look! Here comes the funniest looking girl I ever saw!"

They watched fascinated as the comical figure strode up the path, skirt tail flapping around hairy muscular legs with every unladylike step. At last, with whoops of glee, they recognized Maschinistmaat Bösner. There was no men's clothing in the house he was put in, so when the commander sent word for him to go get a list of all the survivors, he had put on the only dry clothes available. This may well have been the only time in history that a petty officer of the German Navy performed his duty dressed in a skirt and shawl.

By evening, the resourceful 11.WO, Leutnant zur See Herbert Kuhnt, had found German uniforms for all of them, so they entered the mountain troops' camp looking like soldiers instead of masqueraders.

Within a few days they had a message from Admiral Dönitz informing them he had arranged for their transport back to Germany. Once again they put on civilian clothes (no skirts, however) and were taken on a sealed train through Sweden, by steamer to Gotenhafen, and again by train to Wilhelmshaven. They babbled away about their adventures, and were amused by the sight of their commander in knickers and a green hat, and all agreed among themselves that they had had a belly full of U-boat life.

The commander in chief of U-boats, however, had other plans for them. He greeted them with the following speech:

"Comrades, you have been through great difficulties, and it was a splendid achievement that so many of you were able to get off the boat. This experience has forged the crew together even more strongly, and as soon as possible, I will give you a new boat."

It was the U-124.

Chapter Three

SOON AFTER the keel of the U-124 was laid at Deschimag Shipyards in Bremen, the first man of her crew arrived. He was Oberleutnant (Ing.) Rolf Brinker, who was to be the chief engineering officer.

Like the commander, Brinker was well-trained and experienced. He had had two years peacetime training on U-boats, and had made war cruises on board the U-13 and U-9.

He had gained a certain amount of notoriety in the flotilla when he returned to the base at Kiel as chief engineering officer on U-13. The boat had suffered engine damage on patrol, and though Brinker had managed to make repairs, the diesels were far from being in good order. Instead of limping slowly along, however, they paradoxically would run only at top speed.

Ships customarily proceed slowly and with extreme caution through the crowded 100-kilometer-long Kiel Canal which connects the North Sea to the Baltic. Therefore, a signal from the U-13 requesting permission to come through at her top speed was received with little enthusiasm and much skepticism at the base at Kiel. U-boat crews were always in a hurry to go on leave after a war patrol, but this was ridiculous.

Base signaled an emphatic and indignant "No." U-13 then politely asked to be towed in, saying her diesels would not run slower than full speed.

The U-boat was stubbornly insistent during the ensuing signals conversation, and permission was finally granted. She zoomed up to her pier like a speed boat, and skidded to a halt in a flurry of spray and delighted shouts. After docking with a flourish seldom seen in a man-of-war, she was boarded by a grim delegation of engineers from the base. They proceeded to carry out a thorough inspection, and only after they confirmed Brinker's report was he allowed to leave the boat.

Brinker was fascinated by the construction of U-124. As the only officer on hand who would sail on this boat, he was everywhere during the building. Nothing escaped his bright inquiring mind. He memorized every detail of the construction, so when she was finally finished, there was not a nut or bolt in her that her L.I. did not know.

As the boat neared completion, Schulz arrived with the former members of his old crew from U-64. Following them, the new men came to Bremen, and the whole crew was now assembled. She was launched on March 9, 1940, and after her dockyard trials in the Weser River, she was turned over to her commander on June 10, ready for duty with the 2nd U-Flotilla.

The new boat was eagerly inspected by the men who had come from U-64. U-124 was one of the big Atlantic boats, a Type IX B, with the finest weapons and equipment. She had four bow and two stern tubes, and carried 22 torpedoes. There was a 105 mm. cannon on the forecasing, as well as a 37 mm. flak and two 20 mm. twin flak guns placed on the after part of the bridge. She had the most modern type of fire control, and excellent wireless and listening equipment, both a passive sound detector and a type of sonar gear.

Karl Rode, one of the Obermaschinists, had noted with satisfaction that no expense had been spared in the engine room either to give a correspondingly high horsepower in the two main diesels which could deliver 18 knots and the electric motors which gave her a top speed of 7.3 knots underwater. There was no doubt that they had a superb weapon in their hands.

Rode soon discovered, however, that the comforts of the crew had occupied a much lower priority than these technical fittings. Although at 1,100 displacement tons, she was considerably larger than the U-64's 770 tons, Rode had not expected a luxury liner. But he had seen foreign submarines of a comparable size with far more spacious living quarters for their crews.

The German Type IX B, like the VII C's, had bunks for only half the men, so that when a man left his bunk to go on watch, the man coming off crawled in. It was difficult to get about on the boat, for when the watch changed, almost all the 48-man crew would be going from one place to another. There were no hall-like passageways to carry the traffic, so it was channeled through all the main compartments.

During mealtimes, a leaf was raised along the sides of the tables that ran lengthwise through the messes, and this made it almost impossible for anyone to squeeze past. When action stations was called while the men were eating, the resulting bedlam defied description as some 48 men raced simultaneously to their assigned battle posts, leaving a fearsome wake of trampled toes, terrifying sailors' oaths, and smashed crockery. The number of dishes remaining at the end of a cruise was in inverse proportion to the number of alarms sounded at mealtime.

Although certain other creature comforts, such as air conditioning, were conspicuously non-existent in the German boats, the crews did not mind too much. They were well aware that these things were sacrificed in the interests of fighting power and maneuverability, and one chase by a destroyer was all that was necessary to convince a sailor that a little added agility on the part of his boat more than compensated for sharing his bunk. Even the commander had the most spartan accommodations in the tiny cabin that served as office and sleeping space, with only a green curtain to give an illusion of privacy.

But of all the small rooms in a boat not noted for spaciousness anywhere, the most notorious was the toilet. The boat had six torpedo tubes; this room was known as "Tube 7." It was possibly the most complicated piece of equipment on board, and certainly the most temperamental.

To begin with, the user must decide before entering this tiny sanctuary whether he wished to sit or stand. Once inside, there was no room to turn around. After accomplishing his primary mission, he was set to tackle the secondary and most challenging one, that of flushing the toilet.

The rules had to be committed to memory and were specific enough about the order in which he must open and close which valves and operate the pump, and he had been shown how by one of the old hands. But few U-boat toilets were so docile as to allow themselves to be mastered by a novice without kicking up their heels a few times. Nor were they so lacking in individuality as to conform exactly to the rules printed on the instruction sheet. Each one had its own idiocyncrasies that had to be catered to.

It was this characteristic that led to the downfall of any new officer, accustomed to the luxuries of a big ship, who came to a U-boat with a superior or condescending attitude. He was at the mercy of the sailor who gave him his lessons, and who could, at will, omit the special trick or knack that meant the difference between success and failure. The young lieutenant would then emerge from Tube 7 after his first solo attempt, crestfallen and dripping with sweat, to face the knowing smiles of his subordinates.

The commander was inexorable toward everyone, and back he would go for another course of instruction. It was sometimes rather humbling for a highly trained German officer to find that he must have several lessons to learn how to flush a toilet.

In addition to the roguish disposition of these contraptions, there was also the drawback of having only two on board. And one of them was, for all practical purposes, inaccessible during the first part of a patrol since it was located just behind the pantry and blocked by stacks of hams and the beloved German sausages. It could only be called into service after these provisions were used up.

Even this, however, was an improvement over the World War I boats, according to Admiral von Friedeburg, who was a master of story telling. There was only one toilet on board these boats, and it was located just off the galley. To reach it, one had to squeeze past the stove, and the cook had given strict orders that every visitor must give the soup a couple of stirs with the spoon as he went by. The location of the head thus made everyone on board, from the commander on down, an assistant cook.

One further disadvantage of a U-boat's plumbing system was that it could not be used when the boat was being pursued by a destroyer. The noise of flushing it would call attention to their exact position, which would then be clearly marked by a trail of sewage.

But these tribulations lay in the future as the U-124 left her cradle at Bremen bound for Kiel and her shake-down cruise in the Baltic Sea.

The crew worked up well together and the boat was soon over her teething troubles. Schulz was sat-isfied with the results. She handled nicely, and it had not taken him long to get used to the differences between her and his old U-64. She was faster and had more sea endurance, and she carried more torpedoes. He wanted a chance to fire them. Losing the U-64 had been a bitter disappointment to him, and to have lost her without sinking a single ship to compensate for it had made her loss doubly hard to swallow.

Brinker was like a child with a new toy and was constantly finding new ways to play with his treasure. He practiced holding her in trim with every possible combination of the ballast tanks and with the motors and diving planes. He worked out every trick he could dream up to shave a split second or so off their diving time. He invented special adjustments that would give her an extra couple of knots speed in an emergency, and discovered the exact number of revolutions on each electric motor that would give them the most silent creeping speed possible under water.

All these details and many more were stored in Brinker's brain for instant use. He knew that when they were needed, there would not be time to look them up in a book or figure them out. He would have only a split second in which to act, and unless he knew instantly and precisely what to do, it would be too late. By the time the shakedown cruise was over, Brinker knew to a hair what the boat was capable of under every conceivable circumstance, short of an actual depth charging.

This brilliant and unpredictable aristocrat had quickly won the hearts of all the engine room men. He had been the soul of patience and consideration, and he respected and listened to petty officers who were years older than himself. When the young ratings made mistakes, he calmly showed them the right way instead of reprimanding them. He gave his men responsibility and self-confidence, so that both in the control room and the two engine rooms, everything was so well-ordered that the boat seemed to run herself.

It was a pleasant time for all of them. The days were warm and sunny, and they found many hours of swimming and relaxation in the port cities of the Baltic. One particularly memorable evening was spent in the beautiful city of Danzig.

Since U-124 had sleeping space for only about half her men, most of them were billeted on the mother ship while in port, and only a skeleton crew remained aboard the boat.

It was a long, wet, and festive night, despite the fact that the boat was scheduled for her underwater speed trials at seven o'clock the next morning. Around 5 A.M., the crew drifted back to the mother ship, gaily singing, in various stages of sobriety. This gave them a couple of hours to sleep and sober up before stumbling on board the boat.

The officer who was to conduct the trials was on the bridge shortly before seven. A full captain, he had the reputation throughout the flotilla of being exceptionally strict and severe, and his forbidding manner killed any hopes the U-124's bedraggled crew might have had that the rumors were unfounded. They gave him a wide berth, and sat or stood at their posts nursing their hangovers and wishing they were dead.

By seven o'clock, most of them were aboard, though somewhat dilapidated. Several were conspicuous by their absence. The commander had not put in an appearance, nor had Lt. Kuhnt, nor Oblt. Brinker. Of the U-124's four officers, only Lt. Hirsacker was present. He stormed about the boat, nervously shouting unnecessary orders at miserable sailors whose heads were already ringing like gongs.

Seven-thirty came, and someone timidly suggested that perhaps nobody had waked their commander. A messenger was hurriedly dispatched, and a short time later Schulz appeared. He exchanged frigid salutes with the test captain, and went below without saying a word.

He stalked through the boat, checking her readiness to sail. With her hungover crew and only half her complement of officers, she was obviously nowhere near ready to put to sea, and he wondered furiously if that martinet on the bridge had ever seen such a sloppy, disorganized, and don't-give-a-damn boat.

The men watched him apprehensively as he looked from one to the other, his face harsh and his dark eyes black with fury. When he spoke, his voice was low and controlled, but with a chilling and unmistakable undercurrent of anger.

Shortly after eight o'clock, Lt. Kuhnt arrived and reported himself on board, smiling and unsuspecting. His friendly greeting was squelched by an icy stare from his commander, and silence again ruled on the bridge.

The atmosphere was almost as funereal inside the boat as the men spoke in hushed voices or not at all.

"Any sign of Herr Brinker?" Rode asked, coming into the control room.

"No," answered Raudzis, "and it's for sure we can't make a speed trial without the L.I."

"What's the Old Man doing?"

"He's on the bridge, waiting for Brinker, and mad as hell," the *Bootsmann* replied.

"Probably as hung over as we are," Kesselheim added with a smile of malicious satisfaction.

Hermann Kaspers looked up. "Willem's got insides of steel. Anybody else would have gone off like a bomb before now."

"Well, don't start counting your blessings," Rode said. "He can't hold out much longer. I just hope that when he does explode it'll be up there on the bridge and not in the engine room." He turned and started back. "Let us know when and if the L.I. decides to show up. We can at least try to get out of the line of fire!"

Shortly past 8:30, a figure strolled casually down the dock toward the boat. It was Brinker, in civilian clothes, jaunty and unconcerned.

The commander stared at him, transfixed for a moment in stupefied disbelief. Then, his icy composure utterly vanished, and growling an extraordinary oath, he spun on his heel and stormed off the boat. He did not offer a word nor a salute to the four-striper he left standing dumbfounded on the bridge, and marched past Brinker without even acknowledging his existence.

The speed trials were postponed until the following day, and the incident closed with none of the disciplinary disasters the crew expected.

As soon as war was declared, designating numbers had been ordered painted off the conning towers of U-boats because of their value to the enemy. So each boat chose an emblem of her own, to be worn in place of a number. These were highly individualistic, and many became famous.

Everyone knew the raging bull which was painted on Günther Prien's U-47 as he returned from his brilliant and historic penetration of the British naval anchorage at Scapa Flow. The bull was the brain child of his young exec, "Bertl" Endrass, who, later in command of the U-46 and U-567, became one of the best U-boat skippers, wearing the Oak Leaves to the Knight's Cross. He, like Prien, met dazzling success in the Atlantic convoy lanes, and finally death.

And the U-333's three little fishes were already renowned when her commander Ali Cremer brought her all the way across the Atlantic, desperately damaged and unable to dive or even withstand very rough seas, her whole bow caved in from a collision with a freighter he had torpedoed.

When the U-124 returned to Bremen to be checked out after her sea trials in the Baltic, she proudly wore an edelweiss emblazoned on her conning tower. Schulz and the old U-64 crew had adopted the insignia of the Alpine troops that had saved them at Narvik. So now the little flower that only grows high in the Alps was to decorate a U-boat that would roam the ocean depths, and the crew wore a matching insignia sewn on their caps.

The boat proceeded from Bremen to Wilhelmshaven where she was provisioned, and then to her flotilla base at Kiel. From there on August 19, 1940, she passed through the Kiel Canal and, in company with two M-boats (mine sweepers), headed up the North Sea to circle around Scotland and reach her patrol area in the North Atlantic.

The seas were not high, and the sky was fully covered by heavy clouds as the U-124 pushed through the swells. The clouds were a welcome protection from the British aircraft which constantly patrolled the Denmark Straits and the North Sea, and with the exception of the always-alert bridge watch, the crew was relaxed.

Suddenly without the slightest warning, a British bomber roared down out of the massed clouds and dropped four bombs. None of them hit, and while the stunned Germans were still wondering where on earth it had come from and how it had spotted them, it had disappeared again.

The attack was so sudden that no one inside the boat knew what was going on. But the sound of the bombs exploding close by proved too much for one of the youngsters in the control room, and he opened the flooding valve without waiting for orders.

Kuhnt, who had the bridge watch, waited tensely to see if the plane would make another attack. As the angle of the deck suddenly changed beneath his feet, he glanced down to see, to his horror, that the boat was diving, the whole bow already under water.

"Clear the bridge!" he screamed, and dived through the hatch on top of the lookouts. He managed to slam the hatch cover just as the bridge slid under water.

The control room was confusion itself, what with the unordered dive, and the helmsman had unaccountably turned loose the wheel, which lay hard starboard. The commander had run into the control room at the first unexpected motion of the boat, but she had already reached 60 meters by the time he could bring her up.

U-124 surfaced near the two M-boats, none the worse for her adventure. Her U-64 veterans, understandably plane-shy after their ducking at Narvik, stood sheepishly while their commander angrily dressed them down, making it crystal clear that he had no intentions of being drowned by a bunch of addle-headed clowns.

The next day brought more planes and more bombs, until Schulz decided that the two M-boats served to give his position away. He parted company with them, and took his own boat under water for the remaining daylight hours, to be well away from his escort by the time he surfaced again.

The pleasant early autumn days they had left turned abruptly into typical stormy North Atlantic weather as they drew level with the British Isles. North-northwest winds had howled themselves into gales, and the boat was able to make little or no headway into the heavy swells.

It was cold and dark and wet on the bridge as the U-boat plowed through the night. Inside only the men on watch were awake. The commander lay curled up in his bunk, lulled into a peaceful, dreamless sleep by the familiar rocking motion and the steady droning of the diesels. The waves pounded against the bow, splashing spray up to the conning tower, to slide foaming down the length of the hull. Occasionally an object would fall clattering to the deck inside the boat as a big wave shook her. These sounds and movements were so familiar to the commander that he would find it difficult to sleep on shore the first night or two whenever he returned from a patrol.

"Control room!" the I. WO's voice came down from the bridge.

"Control room here," Siegfried Nagorny answered him.

"Wake up the relief. Tell them to wear oilskins."

"Aye, aye, sir."

Nagorny wove his way carefully over and around the stacks of provisions, balancing himself against the rolling of the boat and ducking under hammocks of hard sailors' bread that swung menacingly about head high.

Searching briefly through the tiers of sleeping men, he found the one he wanted and shook him by the shoulder.

"Wakey, wakey, Hänschen."

"Hmmmm?" Hans Fröhlich murmured sleepily. "What's the matter?"

"Time to go on watch."

"Go to hell!"

"Herr Kuhnt refuses to stand his watch without you by his side. So get up."

"Will you go to hell? I'm getting up, so leave me alone," Hänschen grumbled, struggling out of his bunk. "You'd think the whole damn war depended on my not ever getting any sleep!"

"That's right," Siggi returned cheerfully. "Admiral Dönitz himself said so. 'We'll win the war if we can keep Hans Fröhlich out of the sack.' Wake Röhner, will you? And wear your oilskins."

"Oh hurrah. Just what I wanted . . . rain."

Siggi turned and started back to the control room.

"One of these days I'm going to strangle that bastard," Hänschen promised himself solemnly. "Come on, Karl, get up," he said, shaking Karl Röhner, peacefully sleeping in the bunk above him. "Time to go on watch."

"Already?" Karl asked mournfully. "I know I just got to sleep. And I was so nice and warm."

"Well, rise and shine. Lt. Kuhnt's sent us an engraved invitation. He's having a party for us . . . champagne and naked dancing girls."

Hänschen struggled into his heavy foul weather gear. He, like the rest of the crew, slept in his clothes.

"Oh, yes," he went on, "formal dress. Oilskins required."

Karl stopped in mid-yawn. "Oilskins? *Verdammter Scheisz!*"

The petty officer and Lt. Kuhnt were already ahead of them on the bridge.

"Coming up!" Karl called up the ladder to the bridge, and the two climbed quickly up to relieve the lookouts.

The cold winds had whipped the wave tops into driving spray that stung and blinded the men on watch until it was impossible to see anything. Their bodies ached from the strain of balancing themselves against the violent motion of the boat, and they shivered in spite of their heavy clothes.

"Well, that's it," Hirsacker said, completing the formalities of turning over the watch and all its responsibilities to his relief. "Good night and good watch."

"Thank you," replied Kuhnt.

"Good night, Herr Oberleutnant," the new watch chorused.

"Coming down!" Hirsacker called, and the relieved watch clattered down the ladder into the control room.

The commander stirred briefly in his sleep as the watch changed and the passage outside his curtained doorway was filled with hurrying feet and babbling voices. He stirred, almost reached consciousness, then turned over, automatically wedging himself securely against the guard rail, and continued to sleep soundly. For these confused sounds too were part of the normal routine, and they lulled and comforted the commander in his sleep.

The dripping lookouts had sloshed back to the galley to warm up, dry out, and eat bread and sausage.

"Long watch, wasn't it?" Hermann Kaspers remarked, his mouth full.

Willi Gerisch nodded. "It always is when it's raining. I'm half-frozen and half-drowned, and I didn't see a damned thing."

"Me either."

"Hey, Smutje," Willi called to the cook, Adolph Schäfer, "got any coffee?"

"Naturally," answered Schäfer. "Don't I always have fresh coffee when you come off watch?"

The two ate and drank in silence.

"Delicious, Herr Smutje, delicious!" Willi said at last, patting his stomach. "And now for Zizzing Stations! Ready, Hermann?"

"And how. I'm bushed."

They started toward the bow, dragging their dripping rain coats. They reached the bow compartment, full, contented, and drowsy, with no thought beyond collapsing in a nice warm bunk.

But at the entrance, they were brought up short. Every bunk was chained up against the bulkheads, leaving the compartment clear. The doors to the four torpedo tubes were open, and the long evil-looking fish were pulled out with chains and pulleys into the compartment.

"Goddammit to hell, Hannes!" howled Willi. "I want to go to bed!"

Hannes Wiegand glanced up unperturbed. "Now Willi, the torpedoes have to be regulated every two days and you know it."

"Well why in hell don't you do it sometimes when we're on watch?" moaned Hermann. "I'm dead on my feet."

"Oh, you guys quit bitching," Edwin Selk, the torpedo mate said amiably. "If you're in such a hurry you can lend a hand."

Hermann flopped wearily down on one of the torpedoes "I'll be so damn glad when some of these fish get into a Britisher and out of my way," he said.

As though in answer to Kasper's wish, the radio man waked the commander and handed him a signal. Schulz scanned it briefly, then picked up his cap and went into the control room. His finger moved quickly across the chart as he traced his own course and the probable course of the convoy just reported to him.

"Let's go hunting, Hirsacker," he said to the officer at his side. "British convoy—steering in the direction of Cape Wrath."

"That's good news, sir," Hirsacker replied. "Is it close?"

Although the conversation was not audible to the rest of the men in the control room, they watched the commander and first officer, and they knew.

"Come to course 170 degrees," Schulz called, still bending over the chart table. "We'll intercept approximately here," he continued to Hirsacker, tracing the course with his finger, "cut them off by the Butt of Lewis."

"Steering course 170 degrees, sir," the helmsman answered.

"Shadow off the port beam!" a lookout called from the bridge.

Schulz climbed up through the hatch. "Where?"

"Here, sir," Röhner answered, not taking his eyes off the dark shape barely visible.

Schulz watched silently through his binoculars. "Fishing boat," he murmured finally. "But she's headed straight for us. We'd better give way." He leaned over the hatch. "Hard starboard!"

He turned back beside Röhner to watch until the shadow disappeared. Then he brought his boat back on course and left the bridge.

At 2217, the convoy came into sight on the starboard beam, and Schulz turned to hold contact, steaming along parallel to the convoy, keeping the ships in sight while the U-boat herself remained invisible as he plotted their base course and speed.

He gradually circled around and pulled ahead so as to be in position to attack from the front and on the land side.

"Destroyer!" Fröhlich called out behind him on the bridge. "Heading this way!"

Schulz spun around and watched the ship. "Hard port!" he ordered. "Make ready tubes 5 and 6."

Within a few seconds, two torpedoes streaked toward the agile destroyer, already turning away to safety.

Both torpedoes had missed, but the way was clear into the convoy. The wolf was in the sheepfold.

Soon the shadowy forms around them began to take shape as they came on the surface into the main body of the convoy. The four men on the bridge—the commander, I.WO, and two lookouts—stood tense and watchful, eyes and nerves sharply alert as the big merchantmen loomed up around them.

"Take this one, Hirsacker," Schulz said, motioning to a large freighter on their starboard quarter. "Ten degrees starboard," he said into the speaking tube. "Come to course 25 degrees."

Hirsacker bent over the night sight. In a surfaced attack, the I.WO fired the torpedoes while the commander conned the boat. In a submerged attack, the commander did the shooting.

"Target bearing 25 degrees," Hirsacker called out. "Target speed: 10 knots, own speed: 4 knots . . ."

The information was fed into the fire control below and the torpedo set and made ready to fire.

Hirsacker frowned intently into the night sight, as

the freighter moved into the crosshairs. The time was 2350.

"Torpedo one . . ." he called. "Fire!"

The boat lurched slightly as the torpedo left the tube, and for a moment all their attention was on the fish with its load of 350 kilograms of TNT speeding toward the unsuspecting ship.

"Hard port!" the commander called. "This one," he said, pointing toward a freighter some 800 meters away.

Precisely one minute after the first shot, a second torpedo was set and fired.

"Ship bearing dead ahead!" a lookout shouted.

"Shoot her, Hirsacker!" yelled Schulz.

"Target bearing zero degrees," Hirsacker called out. "Set depth at three meters—fire!"

The time was now 2353.

"Hard starboard!" The boat veered sharply away, as Schulz swung her out of the path of the freighter.

"Herr Kaleu," a lookout called, "the first ship we hit is sinking!"

"And the second one is hit amidships, sir!" the other lookout added.

"Try to watch and see if she sinks," Schulz told him. Unless someone actually saw her go down, she could only be reported as a hit.

"Ship on the starboard bow—close!"

"Hard port!" Schulz roared. The freighter looked enormous, her bow sharp and terrifyingly close as she bore down on them on a collision course. "Brinker, full speed emergency! Twice full speed!"

"Will do!" Brinker yelled back, finding nothing outlandish in being ordered to run his diesels at double their top speed.

Brinker's sure touch gave the boat a sudden spurt that got her out of the way of the freighter, which swept past, never even seeing the U-boat she had so nearly rammed.

The convoy was now in the wildest commotion from Schulz's attack. It was impossible to tell whether there was one boat or a dozen, and for the past few minutes it had seemed that torpedoes were coming from every direction.

"Here's a big one, Herr Kaleu!" Hirsacker pointed to a ship just ahead.

"Good," Schulz replied.

At 2356 hours, the fourth torpedo was fired, leaving the four bow tubes empty. It slammed into the merchantman, apparently hitting her engine room, for the ship rolled over and sank almost immediately.

U-124 now found herself outside the awful devastation she had created, as she crossed the outer column of ships. As the men on the bridge caught their breath in the momentary lull, they were suddenly blinded by a destroyer's searchlight turned squarely on the U-boat. For a moment they were as disconcerted as the hapless merchantmen they had ambushed in the darkness.

The destroyer was close and charging like a bull. There was nothing for it but to hit the cellar. And indeed, hope they made it there before this Britisher landed on them like the Avenging Angel.

"Alarm!" yelled Schulz. "Dive! Dive!"

He jumped through the hatch just behind the lookouts.

"Hatch is closed!" he called.

Brinker nodded absently at this piece of information. He had, contrary to all regulations, pulled the plug when he heard the commander's "Alarm" without waiting for reports that the boat was tight. By the time the commander had closed the hatch and reported it to Brinker, the boat was well on her way down, thus saving precious seconds.

This risky habit of Brinker's depended on the absolute reliability of every man involved and allowed no margin for error. Any mistake or failure to make the boat tight would result in flooding her, and with her down angle, it would have been impossible to bring her back up again. Therefore, it was strictly forbidden to dive before the boat was reported tight. Brinker did it all the time.

She was still plunging downward when a powerful shock hit the bow and she ground to a halt. An ominous shudder ran the length of the boat, and likewise through the crew, as she gradually leveled off at 90 meters and hung, still trembling, in the silent waters.

Apprehensive faces turned to the commander in the control room.

"A rock," he answered their unspoken question. "We've hit a rock. Get a damage report from the forward torpedo room, Kuhnt."

The destroyer had meantime reached their position, and she thundered by with a throbbing roar, the whirling screws rising to an unbearable crescendo as she passed over their heads.

Schulz turned to watch Kesselheim at the sound gear. Kesselheim looked up and for a moment their eyes met. Suddenly Kesselheim snatched off the earphones and the commander braced himself firmly against the chart table.

The first series of depth charges went off, rocking the boat wildly and knocking several men off their feet. The commander had been warned by Kesselheim's gesture. He had heard the click of the first depth charge's firing pin and had jerked off the earphones to prevent damage to his eardrums by the explosions which came a split second later.

The boat shuddered and groaned with the impact of the churning water as the depth charges exploded around her. Her crew hung on, breathless and helpless. Schulz gripped the chart table, his handsome face as alert and watchful as a tiger about to spring, and without the slightest trace of fear. His orders were given in a voice that was crisp and confident, and his manner was self-reliant to the point of arrogance.

Fear is contagious, but so is courage. The commander's bearing under fire calmed his men's fears, and they found themselves wondering not so much *if* they would escape, but *how* Willem was going to pull it off.

"Port ten degrees," the commander said. They had come out on the land side of the convoy, and it was too shallow for them to go deep to evade the destroyer. Silence would now be their best defense. "Take her down easy, Brinker, and lay her on the bottom."

"Aye, Herr Kaleu," answered Brinker.

By the time the destroyer had time to turn around and come back, U-124 was lying on the bottom, scarcely 100 meters deep, and quiet as a tomb in response to her commander's order of "absolute silence in the boat." Even the gyrocompass was shut off so its humming would not betray them.

The men involuntarily looked up, their eyes following the sound of the destroyer's screws as she came closer. The pinging of her asdic along U-124's steel flanks clawed at their nerves and cold sweat ran down their bodies as they waited silently.

The pinging grew louder and louder, then gradually began to diminish as the destroyer passed overhead. The depth charges she dropped were not as close as the first pattern, and after one more run, the destroyer's screws faded away for good.

"Bring her up to periscope depth, Brinker," Schulz

said. "The Tommy was too impatient," he added scornfully.

But Schulz knew the danger of being chased by a destroyer in these shallow waters. Had she hunted a little longer, she had stood an excellent chance of blasting them out of the water as the U-boat, denied the security of depth and freedom to maneuver, lay helpless. Schulz had been only too well aware of this as the destroyer had gone over their heads, the cold fingers of her asdic relentlessly probing for them.

The U-boat was alone when she reached the surface. In the distance, a ship burned brightly and a small searchlight flickered nearby. Of the convoy there was nothing else. It had apparently altered course as soon as the U-boat was driven under and was gone. It was over.

When the score was tallied up, it was plain that U-124 was a fighting boat. For the four torpedoes she had fired, she could claim three ships sunk for a total of 17,563 tons, and a further 4,000-ton ship damaged. This one, the British steamer STAKESBY, was torpedoed only 23 miles off the Butt of Lewis, and was towed in.

Schulz would not know the extent of the damage from the rock until three days later, when he spotted another potential victim, a lone blacked-out freighter, and moved into position to attack. He had drawn a bead on the unsuspecting merchantman and was ready to shoot.

"Open outer doors to the forward torpedo tubes," he said, and waited for the usual "outer doors to torpedo tubes open, sir," that meant his order had been carried out. This time it did not come.

"Outer doors won't open, sir!"

"What?" Schulz turned around in surprise.

"The doors seem to be jammed, sir."

Schulz thought for a moment, then, "That damned rock!" he growled.

"Wait, sir," a voice called from the torpedo room. "We've got tube 2 open now, but not number 1."

Schulz checked the periscope again. "Bearing 90 degrees," he called out. "Distance 1000 meters ... set depth at 8 meters ... fire two!"

He watched anxiously as time ran out for the torpedo. "I estimated her speed too high," he muttered.

The freighter was now out of range and soon out of sight, escaping for good in the darkness.

When daylight came, Schulz sent a diver over the side to inspect the damage to the torpedo tubes. Tube 1 would open only a quarter of the way, number 2 was also damaged but would close, number 3 was damaged but would close tightly, and number 4 was undamaged. The diver managed to work the doors into a position that would be safe at up to 40 meters submergence.

The damaged outer doors had made it difficult to attack, and since they would not close tightly, their condition also forbade a deep dive. It was fortunate for them that the destroyer attack had occurred in waters only 100 meters deep, although they had cursed their luck at the time. The pressure at a greater depth would doubtless have flooded the boat.

Schulz wirelessed his situation to headquarters, including the usual report on fuel and torpedoes remaining. Since he had fuel and supplies to last for several more weeks, he was ordered to remain on station as a weather boat, sending back reports at two hour intervals. The Luftwaffe needed weather information in conducting their bombing raids on Britain, and U-boats had been requested to add meteorological data to all their reports.

During the following days, U-124 chased several single-traveling ships, but due to fog, darkness, and her own lack of speed, was unable to make an attack.

Since their main duty now was to report the weather, Schulz, in an effort to keep both morale and efficiency high, drilled his boat and crew with German thoroughness. And if they complained of overwork, they still took pride in their speed and precision. For even the most short-sighted sailor on board understood as well as his commander that the day might come when a split second shaved off a dive or turn might save their lives.

Schulz had earned the respect and admiration of his crew, and they liked him as a man. He was fair and reasonable, adhering to the relaxed discipline characteristic of U-boats; but of infinitely greater importance to them, he was a bold and aggressive fighter. He had dived into that convoy like a hawk into a flock of chickens and had bagged four of them in precisely six minutes.

It was axiomatic in the U-boat service that the popular commander was the successful one, and vice versa. Of all the qualities a crew might want to find in their commander, far and away the most important was the ability to sink ships. The U-124 crew figured their captain for a real professional, smart and experienced. And he had guts.

Officers and men alike quickly found that he demanded the very best from them. But he was easy to get along with, witty and cultured, and he was a first-rate seaman. He had a keenly intelligent mind and a great deal of self-discipline, which the officers and petty officers in the control room especially welcomed during an attack. They were well aware that some U-boat skippers drove their men frantic setting up an attack by constantly calling for new firing data to be calculated. Every time the target bearing shifted, they would sing out a new set of figures to be worked out. Frequently they would have a dozen sets of calculations and an exhausted group of control room personnel by the time the first torpedo was fired.

Alternatively, Schulz would wait as long as possible to have the settings calculated, then would work out any subsequent changes in his head and compensate for them when he fired. The result was a calm, orderly, and efficient attack that could be carried out at great speed. And his shooting was exceptionally accurate.

The night was quiet as U-124 plodded aimlessly through the cold rough waters of the North Atlantic some 500 sea miles west of the Hebrides. She had just sent her latest weather report, intercepted one from Prien in U-47, and had nothing to do until the next one. Half the crew, including the commander, were asleep while the other half stood their watches. Karl Rode had the "dog watch" in the (electric) engine room.

The petty officer on watch in the control room, the Zentralemaat, suddenly remembered that he had received a complaint concerning Tube 7.

"Hi, Grigoleit!" he called to a machinist. "Go aft and see if there's anything wrong with Tube 7. And while you're about it, give the mechanism a good oiling."

The easy-going young East Prussian, nicknamed Grigoleit, promptly marched back to take care of it. He nodded cheerfully to Rode as he went by.

A few silent minutes passed, then the door was flung open and Grigoleit, white-faced and wild-eyed, emerged screaming, "The boat's flooding!"

He was soaked from head to toe, both with the contents of Tube 7 and the cold Atlantic, which was indeed, pouring in with a vengeance. He ran to Rode, still yelling and waving his arms frantically.

Rode had needed no one to tell him the boat was flooding. Tube 7 lay several meters under the surface, and the sound of water streaming in under pressure brought back that awful day at Narvik with such horrifying clarity that he shuddered involuntarily. He could only think, "Oh no! Not our new boat!"

He grabbed Grigoleit, who was still clutching something in his right hand. Rode recognized it instantly as the stopcock from Tube 7, which should have been turned but not removed. In his haste and confusion, Grigoleit had unfortunately held onto it.

Rode snatched it out of his hand and dashed into the tiny compartment. It took only seconds to push it back in place and stop the flow of cold Atlantic water, and only a little longer to pump out that which had come in.

There would be many a good laugh in the months to come over the foolish look on Grigoleit's face and the agitation he had so innocently managed to cause. But beneath their laughter was the grim awareness that if it had happened while the boat was submerged, no human strength could have shoved the stopcock back in place against the pressure of the ocean.

The commander found the whole episode something short of hilarious. He had been awakened from a sound sleep by the blood-chilling scream, "The boat's flooding!" He hit the deck at a dead run, not knowing what catastrophe he was facing. He raced frantically toward the sound of the water, but by the time he arrived at the scene of the crime, Rode's quick action had ended the crisis.

Shaken and furious, he berated the Zentralemaat who was supposed to see to the repairs in terms that were eloquent, forceful, and 100 per cent Navy, and retired to his cabin with a cup of coffee, still swearing under his breath.

The Zentralemaat listened meekly to his commander's tirade, then proceeded to pass it on to the luckless Grigoleit.

Her fuel and supplies nearly expended, U-124 was at last ordered to return to base. Her crew were now full-fledged veterans, steady and competent. They knew their boat intimately and regarded her with warm affection. She seemed to take an unholy delight in throwing an occasional scare into them, but she could always be counted on to give a little more speed and quickness than her designers had built into her. By the end of the cruise, every man aboard was sure their "little steamer" was the finest ship on the ocean.

An unexpected piece of good news accompanied their orders home. France had fallen, and U-boat bases were now established along the Bay of Biscay. Instead of returning to Kiel, U-124 was to report to the new headquarters of the II U-Flotilla at Lorient.

Chapter Four

SHORE LEAVE in France! French food—French wine—French *girls*! Life was suddenly and incredibly magnifique!

No more watches to stand, no more stinking U-boat air to breathe. The rough sea and dangerous fighting were gone . . . for the duration of this leave, at least. The destroyers and their depth charges were far away, although they continued to haunt their dreams and would for years to come.

For most of the crew, it was their first trip to France and they could hardly wait to plunge into the welcome task of forgetting the war. The heady French wine cost no more than German beer, and champagne and cognac were within the means of everyone.

The French people seemed pleasant and hospitable, and the language barrier proved to be no problem. Smiles and arm waving served the purpose at the beginning, and in a few months, both the French and Germans picked up a working knowledge of the other's language.

The U-boat crews, deliriously glad to be safe on

shore, drank wine and sang in the cafés; and if the proprietors were more interested in German money than German laughter and songs, these happy sailors did not know it.

But the first thing every U-boat man wanted when he returned from a patrol was a real bath with tons of hot soapy water to wash away the sweat, grime, and weariness of the North Atlantic. With the limited quantity of fresh water carried on board, a bath at sea was, of course, out of the question. And after several weeks on board a crowded U-boat, a sailor was likely to regard a bath as the nicest thing that could happen to him. The second nicest thing would be for all the other 48 men to have baths.

The crew was quartered in a local hotel provided for "Hein Seemann," and French women did their laundry for a reasonable fee. The men were impressed, and a little surprised, by their scrupulous honesty, having somehow assumed it was an exclusively German virtue. They soon discovered that money, chocolate, and any personal valuables could be left in their rooms in complete safety.

Karl Rode, accompanied by several shipmates, spent the first night on shore making a boisterous round of bars, cafés, night clubs, and the red light district.

In this first reconnaissance of Lorient, they discovered what was to be their favorite haunt, a small and respectable café near the waterfront. It was not the convenient location, however, that made it the Number One Café in the city to them, nor was the price of wine any cheaper. It was entirely because of the lovely girl who worked behind the bar.

They soon found out that her name was Franziska, and also, alas, that she was engaged to be married. She was scarcely 20 years old, and so gay and sparkling that the U-124 men were at once under her spell. They agreed among themselves that if Franziska wanted a German husband instead of a French one, she could certainly have her choice of them!

Rode came to regard this little café as his special Lorient home, and he always headed straight to it as soon as he left the boat. He would be welcomed with hugs and handclasps from the proprietors and a sunny smile from Franziska. It made him feel deliciously warm and comfortable to be thus greeted after the hardships and perils of a war cruise, and to know that someone in this alien city was glad to see him and to know he was alive and safe.

"Bonjour, Monsieur Charlie," she would say to the smiling German, still unshaven and in his leather sea clothes. "Retour Atlantik? Tommy nix boom boom?"

"Oui, Franziska," he would laugh. "Compliments, Madame."

U-124 underwent a short overhauling at the dockyard in Lorient while her crew went on leave, and put to sea on her second war cruise on October 5.

Among the new men for U-124 was a replacement for Kuhnt, the second officer. He was Reinhardt Hardegen, who would later make a name for himself as ace commander of the U-123, and would strike the first blows of the U-boat arm in American waters.

Hardegen opened what came to be known as the "American Shooting Season" on January 12, 1942, by sinking the British freighter CYCLOPS just off the approaches to New York harbor, and later that same night the tanker NORNESS south of Long Island.

His prodigious sinking score up and down the coast within sight of American cities would win him the Knight's Cross and the accolades of his countrymen when he returned to Germany and a hero's welcome.

In company with U-28, U-48, and U-101, U-124

followed a mine sweeper out through the German mine fields to about the 50-meter curve, arriving there just at dark. Then with cries of "Good luck" and "Happy hunting," the escort turned back to Lorient, her mission done.

U-124 now proceeded independently, full speed and on the surface, zig-zagging rapidly. She reached the 200-meter curve by dawn, then submerged. By day she would travel underwater in this heavily patrolled area, surfacing only to recharge her batteries until she reached a longitude of 15 degrees. Having arrived at this pre-arranged point, she would send her first wireless message to headquarters.

I. WO Hein Hirsacker had the bridge watch as the boat pounded steadily through the long swells. Visibility was good on this moonlit night, and he and his men attentively searched the sea around them for any sign of booty or danger.

"Shadow off the starboard bow," a lookout reported.

Hirsacker swung his binoculars around to pick out the small superstructure, visible only because of the moon light glinting on the metal. In the deceptive light, Hirsacker failed to identify the British submarine.

"Destroyer!" he yelped. "A L A R M!"

The bridge watch dived through the hatch, Hirsacker right behind them, slamming the cover over his head. The boat was already tipped over in a down angle as he slid down the ladder into the control room. Within 30 seconds of the time the diving alarm sounded, she had reached a depth of 60 feet.

"High speed screws approaching!" the boy at the sound gear reported. He listened carefully a moment longer, then yelled, "Torpedo!"

The high-pitched whine of the small fast screws

was already clearly audible in the control room. The men looked up in fascinated horror as the sound grew louder and louder. It reached a peak as the two deadly fish passed directly over the conning tower above their heads, then rapidly diminished in the swirling water. It had been close.

"The Tommy's aim was good," the commander said, with grudging professional admiration. "If we'd dived a second later, Hirsacker, he'd have hit us for sure."

He turned back to the business at hand. The British submarine had missed her shot at them, but she had dived too, and now began an eerie cat and mouse game as the two adversaries hunted each other cautiously in the dark, guided only by their ears.

"Brinker, make those motors *whisper*," the commander ordered. "I want *absolute* silence in the boat. Don't even breathe!" he warned the crew.

As silence enveloped the German boat, they could hear the sounds of screws close off the starboard beam.

"Port easy," Schulz said softly.

"Port easy," the helmsman answered.

The boat swung slowly to port. It was impossible to tell the exact position of the other submarine, or her exact course. Schulz had altered his own course only a little, because any abrupt changes would make it easier for the enemy to pinpoint his position.

The British boat was so close now that the sound gear was not needed to hear her. Sounds of her screws, as well as that of her crew moving about came quite clearly through the U-124's steel hull, and the Germans stood, wide-eyed and motionless, not daring to breathe. Was she above or below them? Could she hear them? Would the two blind hunters collide, and so kill each other?

"Midships," the commander whispered.

"Midships."

The U-boat came back to her course, as silent as a shark gliding through the dark waters. The sounds from the other boat were now less distinct, and in a few moments they had faded altogether. The ghostly encounter had lasted only a few minutes and was typical of the appalling swiftness with which one's fortunes could change on a U-boat.

Schulz's operational area was south of Iceland in the North Atlantic, and long before these waters were reached, the crew had settled into the accustomed routine of a war cruise.

It was October 16, eleven days since they had put out from Lorient. They had just eaten lunch, with chocolate pudding, the crew's favorite dessert. Those off watch were lazily talking or playing cards, or sleeping. The commander and L.I. were playing chess in the wardroom. Brinker had just taken his commander's bishop.

"Has anybody reported a convoy in the last week or so?" Brinker asked.

The commander shook his head. "No. Several single ships have been sunk in the Western Approaches, but nobody has picked up a convoy."

"I'd like to know where they're all hiding."

"So would I."

Brinker captured the commander's queen and grinned at him triumphantly.

"Hmmm," Schulz grunted noncommittally. "One battle doesn't mean the war, Brinker," he murmured innocently, but with a wicked gleam in his eye.

"Which way do you think they're sending their ships? This far north?" Brinker asked.

Schulz nodded. "As close as they can to the pack ice, I'd say."

His hand moved over the chess board and came to rest on his knight. "Don't be too impatient. I think we'll find some of them soon." He moved the knight. "Checkmate."

Brinker's mouth flew open at the unexpected move. He stared at the board a moment, then recovered. "You realize, of course, the only reason I let you win is because you outrank me?"

"A likely story!" Schulz grinned smugly. "My Clausewitz-type tactics are just too much for you!"

He rose and stretched. "I'm going up on the bridge. Maybe we can scare up a target."

"I'm coming too," Brinker said. "I want a cigarette."

Since a U-boat's ventilating system did not allow for any additional drain on the air, smoking was forbidden inside the boat. One or two men at a time could come on the Wintergarten (the after part of the bridge), but when the weather was rough or the enemy close, the best a man could do was to wait his turn in the conning tower for a few hasty puffs on a cigarette. And then he stood a better than good chance of being wetted down by an occasional wave pouring through the hatch over his head.

Brinker picked up his pack of cigarettes and followed the commander to the bridge. He liked the commander. It was sometimes very difficult to convince a German naval officer that engines will not necessarily take orders like men. While one might ask for and get superhuman effort from his men, machines are somewhat different. No amount of orders, demands, or threats could make the slightest difference to the two diesels in the engine room, and it was a wise commander who understood that simple fact.

Schulz was no engineer, but he had a natural aptitude for mathematics and machinery. He could readily understand the things Brinker explained to him, and, what was more important, he had complete confidence in Brinker's ability and judgment as an engineer. This made for an excellent working relationship between the two men and a smooth running boat that would have been impossible under a commander who constantly nagged his officers and men.

Visibility was good. There was a cloud bank behind them, and an occasional cloud scudded across the sun. A light wind kicked up whitecaps along the wave tops. Ideal conditions for an underwater attack, the commander registered automatically.

"Have you seen anything, Hardegen?" he asked the watch officer.

"I don't know, sir," Hardegen answered. "I thought I caught a glimpse of a mast peak a minute ago."

"I saw something too," Willi Klein said. "Almost dead ahead. Just a little to starboard."

"A beer for you, Willi, if you find it again," the commander said.

"There!" Willi shouted. "Five degrees! Mast peak!"

"Good boy!" Schulz said, searching with his binoculars. "There. I see it now."

They watched the tiny black thread grow taller on the horizon.

"Clear the bridge," Schulz ordered. "Stand by to dive."

He waited until the bridge watch started down, then followed.

"Periscope depth, Brinker, and hold her steady."

Schulz watched at the attack periscope for a moment, then stepped back. "Down scope," he said. "She's headed this way all right, and zig-zagging. So she's a belligerent and fair game for us."

Brinker stood behind his planesmen, watching the dials and gauges over their heads, giving brief orders now and then. The forward and after ballast tanks had to be alternately flooded and blown, and the angle of the diving planes constantly adjusted to counter the effect of the swells and keep the boat level in the water and exactly at the depth the commander called for. So skilled and precise was their control that the boat could be held almost to the exact inch of the ordered depth.

Schulz continued to make short observations through the periscope, noting masthead height, inclination, bearing, and zig-zag pattern. This information would be fed into the fire control, which would then calculate the exact torpedo settings.

A torpedo travels relatively slowly, so it was necessary to lead the target by a considerable angle. And for the same reason, it was almost imperative that the U-boat be ahead of, or at least abreast, the target ship. A torpedo that had to outrun its target was hopelessly handicapped unless she was close.

The large distances involved would amplify even the slightest miscalculation in the speed of the target or the angle on the bow so greatly as to eliminate all chance of a hit. Irregular zig-zagging and speed changes on the part of a ship also enormously increased the problems of an attacking boat and the chance for the target's escape.

Below Schulz in the control room, Obersteuermann Hagemann bent over the chart table making a plot from the figures the commander called down to him.

"Both half speed," Schulz said. "Come to course one-o-degrees. Make ready tubes 1 and 2."

The outer doors to the torpedo tubes were opened and the tubes flooded. All that remained now was for the mixers to set the torpedoes for speed, course, and depth. They waited for the figures from the commander.

One more careful look, then Schulz sang out the

torpedo settings. He watched the freighter's bow come into the crosshairs of the periscope.

"Torpedo one ..." Now the tiny cross lay precisely on her bridge, amidships. "Fire!"

The vents were opened to flood the trimming tanks in the bow to compensate for the loss of the torpedo's weight. In a few seconds the boat was again trimmed.

"Torpedo running," from Kesselheim at the hydrophones.

Schulz waited. If this torpedo missed, he would fire the second one in an instant. He seldom fired spreads, especially for a single-traveling ship like this one. He could carry only a limited number of fish on a patrol, and saw no point in shooting two or three when one would do. One torpedo, properly placed, would usually sink a ship, and if it did not, he could still shoot another one. Three misses did no more damage than one, and he preferred to put his trust in his sharp aim and good shooting eye, rather than fire a spread of three in the hope that one might hit. His shooting score bore out his theory, and it was a lucky ship that got away once "Willem" got his sights on her.

Hagemann glanced up from the stopwatch he held in his hand. He was timing the torpedo's running time, and from that the commander could check his own estimate of the distance.

"Up scope," Schulz motioned. Then, "Hit!" he yelled. "She's hit aft!"

The crew broke into cheers. Throughout the chase, they had followed what was going on by the series of orders for speed and course and orders to the men in the torpedo compartment. But they could only visualize what was going on on the surface.

Each man had played his part in sending the torpedo crashing through the hull of the merchant ship some 900 meters away, but of them all, only the commander had actually seen their victim.

"Ship is signaling," Fritz Rafalski called from the wireless shack. "S-s-s for submarine. She's the British TREVISA."

"Look her up," Schulz told Hardegen. "Keep listening, Rafalski," he called.

"S-I-N-K-I-N-G . . ." Rafalski spelled out slowly.

"TREVISA is a British freighter, 1,813 tons," Hardegen reported.

The U-boat now cleared out to a respectable distance to wait for the ship to sink. Schulz knew her distress signal would alert any destroyers or planes in the vicinity, and he did not want to be too close in case of visitors. In a short while, she rolled over and sank.

Schulz, watching through the periscope, sighed softly as she went under. He was too much a seaman ever to be able to watch a ship go down without a pang of sadness.

"Brinker!" he called. "Surface!"

The bridge watch stood by the conning tower ladder waiting for the word to go up. Compressed air drove the water out of the ballast tanks and the boat rose swiftly.

Brinker watched the depth gauges. "Conning tower clear, sir."

Schulz threw open the hatch and climbed quickly out. He looked all around. It was clear. "Blow out main ballast by diesel! Bridge watch up!"

The two diesels roared into life, and the boat sprang ahead. The lookouts took their places.

"Come to course one four o! Both ahead full!" Schulz called.

Some three hours later, three destroyers came in sight, apparently searching for the sunken ship. U-124 stayed well out of sight as she cautiously watched them.

Just before nightfall, another destroyer appeared out of a rain squall to pound them with depth charges in payment for the TREVISA. The boat was not damaged and managed to slip away after a short chase.

They continued to sight the fast, zig-zagging single ships at intervals. A lot of skill and patience and work went into a chase between the time a mast tip was sighted on the horizon and a torpedo was launched. And some luck was necessary too. A fast ship could outrun a U-boat, and if darkness fell before the boat could circle around to get into a forward position to shoot her torpedoes, it was hopeless. But U-Schulz had her share of luck and the Allied merchantmen continued to fall before her torpedo tubes and her commander's deadly aim.

Inevitably, too, the destroyers appeared. Sometimes too suddenly for the boat to get away without being detected, and then there would be a duel of wits between Schulz and the destroyer captain.

The U-boat would creep silently along keeping either her bow or stern toward the destroyer so as not to give a broadside target to the searching asdic beams.

The asdic impulses, sent out from a dome on the bottom of the destroyer, would bounce off the U-boat's hull. The frequency and strength of these echoes would betray the boat's position, depth, and distance to a skilled operator, and depth charges would be set and dropped accordingly.

And always, when the depth charges got closer, a U-boat would seek shelter in greater depth. As the commanders drove their boats down past their test depths to escape the exploding Wabos (Wasserbomben—depth charges), the pressure hulls would creak and moan, and the crews would make grim jokes about how soon they would reach "paper depth" (the depth at which the water pressure would crush the hull and so flatten the cigar-shaped boat into the shape of a newspaper).

At first the U-boats would go below the maximum depth charge settings, but then the British caught on and remedied this oversight. Later, boats were sometimes damaged by the powerful "killer" depth charges at depths up to 650 feet.

Von Tiesenhausen, thanks to a faulty manometer (depth gauge), once took his U-331 to a depth of 266 meters, roughtly 730 feet, for an unofficial and hair-raising record dive. This was later topped by 20 feet by Bauer in U-126 when his boat withstood a pressure of 336 pounds per square inch in the deepest dive recorded by a IX C boat.

On October 20, U-124 made contact with the outgoing Convoy OB 229. By dark she had reached a position for a surfaced attack, and sank the Norwegian freighter CUBANO and the Britisher SULACO.

Schulz was bringing his boat back into the convoy on the port side when a lookout behind him yelled, "Destroyer on the starboard quarter!"

One glance was all Schulz needed. "Alarm!" he shouted.

This escort had spotted them and was charging up at full speed.

"2A plus 60,[1] Brinker!" Schulz called out, tumbling down the ladder into the control room.

Water rushed into the diving tanks as Brinker pushed her down at full speed, but the confused noise of diving was suddenly drowned out by the

---

1. A equals 80 meters; thus 2A plus 60 is 220 meters.

destroyer close above them. Her throbbing and whirling screws filled the boat with an insane din, then
the first pattern of depth charges exploded around
the boat, dangerously close. Men already hanging on
to balance themselves against the steep down angle
were knocked off their feet as the boat pitched and
plunged in the wrenching shock of the exploding
Wabos. The commander was thrown to his knees and
he grabbed frantically at a leg of the chart table as
Hardegen slammed into him.

The boat steadied herself after the explosions and
held her nose down to reach a safer depth. The men
picked themselves up and scrambled back to their
posts. They could already hear the destroyer returning.

This time she was moving at a slower and more
deliberate pace, and the pinging of her asdic lashed
the U-boat's steel hull with a maddening rhythm.

"2A plus 60, Herr Kaleu," Brinker reported as they
reached the depth Schulz had ordered.

"Good," the commander said. "Port easy."

"Port easy," Willi Klein answered, turning the
wheel steadily.

Now the destroyer was overhead. The men waited
with sweat streaming down their faces, involuntarily
looking up, following in their minds the death-dealing
canisters as they rolled off the destroyer's fantail to
fall through the water above their heads.

The first explosion was even closer than those in
the first pattern had been. The lights flickered and
went out as glass cracked and shattered in the control
room. The sudden darkness magnified the terrifying
feeling of utter chaos. A sharp cry of pain was lost in
the second explosion and the boat rocked violently.
Each depth charge seemed closer than the one before

it, pounding men and boat with such ferocity that it seemed impossible for the pressure hull to hold.

Then the destroyer was past again, and red lights flickered on in the control room. Broken glass and shredded cork lay everywhere as men, dazed and hurt, staggered to their feet.

Brinker checked the instruments that were still working and gave quick instructions to his men as they brought the quivering boat back under control.

One of his men sagged weakly against the control board and Brinker pulled him around. He was holding his cut hand tight against him as blood dripped down his shirt and onto the deck.

"Goder!" roared Brinker. "Hey, Doctor!"

"I'm coming!" called Goder.

He reached them just as the next pattern of Wabos went off, and he and Brinker clung to each other and to the injured man. The boat tumbled crazily in the swirling water, finally righting herself as the explosions stopped.

"Brinker, take her down another five meters, silent running," the commander said. Then turning to Kesselheim at the sound gear, "Give me the destroyer's bearing and range."

For the next five hours, Schulz maneuvered the boat carefully in a desperate effort to lose the hunter above him. But she seemed almost to anticipate every evasive move he made, returning after each run with her nerve-shredding asdic and the mauling explosions that tore at the boat with savage force.

"Five meters deeper, Brinker," he said.

"Herr Kaleu, we're eight meters below test depth now," Brinker told him.

"I know it," Schulz replied. "But she can't take much more of this. These goddamned Wabos are beating her to death. Take her down another five."

"Aye," replied Brinker.

Looking across the control room, Schulz caught the frightened glance of a young seaman who was on his first patrol. Fear had made him look even younger than he was.

The commander suddenly smiled. "Don't worry," he said. His voice was surprisingly warm and gentle and carried clearly to all of them in the compartment. "I'll bring you home again." His confident grin included all of them. "What would your mothers say if I didn't bring you home again?" For a moment the destroyer did not seem quite so close.

The air was thick, foul, and stifling inside the boat, and Schulz issued potassium cartridges. The men put them in their mouths, and as they breathed through them, the potash helped to remove the carbon dioxide from the air.

And still the pinging asdic pulsed through the steel hull and set their raw nerves to screaming. They knew that when the steadily rising sound reached a peak, it was soon followed by the mauling concussion of the Wabos.

Schulz ordered the boat deeper and deeper, until she crept through depths never dreamed of by her builders, her tough pressure hull holding out the tons of water that threatened to crush her like an egg shell. Water spewed in through seams and pipe joints as tons of pressure sought out every weak spot.

At last he dared not take her a meter lower. Those of the crew not actually doing anything were sent to their bunks to lie down and so conserve the oxygen in the boat. And despite the danger, one by one, they dropped off to sleep.

The men in the control room looked to the officers for reassurance. Schulz and Brinker talked quietly, their faces and voices unexcited, betraying none of the cold fear that clutched at them both. They gave the impression of normalcy and security to the men around them, for the commander and L.I. would surely not stand there gabbing away about God-knew-what if they were about to be blasted to atoms.

Actually, the conversation made no sense at all since Schulz and Brinker were talking about different subjects, but this did not matter since neither was listening to either himself or the other.

The cold-blooded courage that would later make Hardegen a great U-boat commander was already obvious as he roamed through the boat, checking the damage and supervising repairs. His blue eyes were calm and unafraid, and men who might have panicked were strengthened by the young officer who controlled his own fear so completely, talking and joking with the men as they worked.

The attack went on relentlessly through the night and into the next day, and still Schulz could not shake off the destroyer. The situation in the U-boat was becoming critical. The air in the boat was almost suffocating with the ever-increasing carbon dioxide and ever-decreasing oxygen. The batteries were dangerously low, although all non-essential machinery had been shut down hours ago and the screws turned only enough to allow control of the boat. The men off duty lay limp, more unconscious than asleep, and those on watch were almost too weak to stand.

Schulz knew he had to bring the boat up soon or not at all. The destroyer appeared to have lost her sure contact on the boat, but she still hunted, dropping depth charges at random. At last he told Brinker to release some fuel oil. They would try to trick the destroyer into thinking she had made a kill.

Brinker added a couple of gloves and a shoe to the oil which floated to the surface, hoping to give authenticity to the charade, and the destroyer once more passed slowly overhead as she inspected the decoy. Then, having lost the boat on asdic and apparently accepting the evidence of a mortal wound, the destroyer turned, her screws whirling to high speed as she left.

Schulz waited a little longer, then cautiously brought his exhausted boat and crew to the surface. They were alone.

"Did you notice anything strange about that depth charging?" Kesselheim asked Fritz Rafalski later that evening.

"Yes," answered Rafalski shortly. "We're still alive."

"I mean besides that. Remember what we had for dessert yesterday?"

"What are you talking about, Sherry?" Rafalski asked, puzzled and more than a little exasperated. "We had chocolate pudding for dinner ... and Wabos for supper!"

"That's what I mean! Chocolate pudding and Wabos. And day before yesterday ... chocolate pudding and Wabos." Kesselheim was dead serious. "And remember that destroyer that came up out of the fog last week? I still had a mouth full of chocolate pudding when the Old Man pulled the plug."

Rafalski sat thoughtful and silent for a moment. Then he said slowly, "You know, Sherry, I believe you're right."

The case was clinched three days later when chocolate pudding was again on the menu. Right on schedule, a destroyer arrived out of nowhere to plaster them with depth charges.

"That did it!" announced Rafalski as soon as it was over, and marched straight to his commander.

"Herr Kaleu'nt," he said, "I must talk to you."

Schulz turned around, surprised by the urgent tone. "Of course, Rafalski. Come on in my cabin."

He turned and led the way. "Now sit down and tell me what's on your mind."

He listened soberly to Rafalski's story and saw nothing ridiculous or hysterical in it.

U-124 would be depth charged many more times in her life, but chocolate pudding was never again served on board.

Sailors are traditionally a superstitious lot, and the edelweiss boat was not the only one to court Lady Luck. The U-48, under the command of Vaddi Schultze, steered only courses divisible by 7 when in open waters.

When Lt. Bleichrodt later succeeded Schultze as commander, it puzzled him to give a steering order, only to have an entirely different number of degrees repeated to him by an unconcerned helmsman. He repeated his order, and received the same reply. Once again, he repeated his order, this time his voice crackling with anger, only to hear the agreeable voice of the helmsman give back his same original reply.

The unnerved and infuriated Bleichrodt was about to give his crazy new crew a thundering lesson in German Naval discipline when someone explained to him about the U-48's peculiar steering habits. The course he had given was not divisible by 7, so the helmsman had merely chosen the nearest number to it that was, and this was the course he called back to his now nearly apoplectic new commander.

It is worth noting that Bleichrodt conformed to the boat, and not vice versa. Other boats clung just as tenaciously to their own magic formulas and witches' brews as they tried to charm the fates and beat the odds against them.

On October 31, U-124 met a single-traveling

freighter, the British RUTLAND. Attacking on the surface after dark, Schulz fired one torpedo which hit forward. The ship went down in about 30 seconds, followed by a great explosion, presumably her boilers bursting.

The next day he attacked the EMPIRE BISON and sent her to the bottom.

An ocean tug with a yellow stack and one mast was the object of a prolonged chase on November 6. The U-boat sighted her and gave chase, but she suddenly altered course and disappeared.

Schulz dived to listen, then set out toward the sound of her screws. The tug came in sight again briefly, but again slipped away as the U-boat tried to close in.

The last trace of her was an intercepted radio signal, "Submarine appeared again," followed by a position report which precisely located U-124. The tug had escaped.

At last, fuel and supplies almost exhausted, Schulz set his course for Lorient. Boat and crew had acquitted themselves well and they turned toward their base in a holiday mood. Little flags, each bearing the name and tonnage of a ship they had sunk, were sewn and made ready to fly in triumph when they entered port.

The commander slaved over his war diary and patrol reports while his officers diligently struggled with their own paper work. No one wanted to risk so much as a minute's delay in leaving the boat, so nothing was left to chance.

Upon reaching a pre-arranged point, Schulz signaled headquarters, then proceeded to the rendezvous point where he would be met by a mine sweeper to escort him through the German mine fields.

The boat had almost reached her pick-up point,

traveling submerged because of frequent British air patrols. An air of well-being pervaded the boat. The patrol had been successful; they were safe and almost home. The usual games of skat and chess were in full swing.

Suddenly a metallic clang came from the bow of the boat. The crew was used to a thousand noises a day, of infinite variety, and took no notice of them. This sound was different. It was metal striking the outside of the hull, and it froze every man in his tracks.

The ace of spades dropped from Hagemann's nerveless fingers and fell unnoticed to the deck. The cutthroat skat game in progress between him, Leo Raudzis, and Arthur Piepenhagen was suddenly a million miles away.

In the wardroom, Hardegen's elaborate chess strategy was forgotten and he gripped the bishop in his hand until his knuckles were white. When he started to put it down later, he would have no notion where it had been nor what move he had planned to make with it.

Hannes Wiegand, startled into forgetting one of the first lessons he had learned on U-boats months ago, sat bolt upright in his bunk, dealing himself such a blow on the head that he would wonder next day how he had gotten such a knot.

Werner Böhme, a torpedo mixer, was pouring himself a cup of hot coffee. It overflowed the cup onto his hand. He did not even feel the burn until later.

The unspoken word was like a shriek through the length of the boat: M I N E !

The cable scraped slowly along the boat's steel hull. God in Heaven—to be blown up by a mine only hours from port! Cold sweat broke out on faces turned toward the invisible rasping sound. Men did not dare to breathe. Any second the mine would blast them into eternity. Any second now—

The horrible grating moved aft, every second of its progress interminable, unendurable. And suddenly it was gone. Silence. A timorous, questioning whisper through the boat—safe? Then the wild exultation that swept through her entire length—SAFE !

Chapter Five

ADMIRAL KARL DÖNITZ, while still a watch officer on U-boats in World War I, had seen with prophetic insight the immense potential of a powerful submarine force in controlling the seas.

Contrary to the general belief that asdic had spelled the doom of the undersea raider, Dönitz was convinced that the real age of the submarine was yet to come. Asdic and the convoy system had defeated the U-boats of World War I, but neither one was foolproof, and his nimble mind had already concocted ways to get around both.

Asdic was unquestionably a danger, but he did not believe it was more than a match for a good U-boat, skillfully handled. Variations in temperature and salinity of the strata of water tended to distort the asdic impulses, and it was not easy for a searcher to pin-point a U-boat's position precisely. A depth charge had to explode within a few feet of a boat to rupture the pressure hull.

And as a destroyer made her run, there was a short space ahead of her which was dead for her asdic; thus contact was lost during this last crucial moment.

In this short time, if a U-boat skipper had judged it correctly, he might make a sudden evasion that could not be detected on board the hunter above him.

Furthermore, and most important, asdic was useful only for detecting a submerged boat. As long as she remained on the surface, a boat was safe from this device, and the observant watch officer in World War I had already discovered that a U-boat on the surface at night is practically invisible, even at close range.

The tactics he devised were based on the surfaced night attack. He trained his commanders to stay on the surface, safe from the escorts' asdic, and wait for their chance to slip by them into the main body of the convoy. Once inside, they could choose their targets and fire from close range at several ships in rapid succession. A few boats thus attacking the same convoy could do enormous damage while remaining comparatively safe themselves on the surface in the midst of the merchant ships.

Even the brilliant "star shells" fired by the convoy ships did not always reveal the U-boats, since the fitful shadows on the moving water did as much to conceal the low-lying boats as the harsh light did to expose them.

His strategy was culminated in the devastatingly effective group attacks in which a handful of boats could cut a convoy to ribbons, leaving the escorts helpless against the savagery of their onslaught.

Each boat in a wolf pack would be given the code name of his group, so that he might decipher all messages addressed to the group as well as to him individually, for the pack was controlled by the BdU (Befehlshaber des U-Bootes—commander in chief of U-boats: Dönitz) from his headquarters.

The B-Service, Naval Cryptographic Service, succeeded in breaking several British codes, and this proved an effective aid in locating convoys. Whenever the B-Service reported a convoy to Dönitz, he would study the operational map which covered one wall and on which the position of each U-boat at sea was represented by a pin. He would indicate on the map the expected course of the convoy, and then deploy the nearest wolf pack into a reconnaissance line across it. He would try to place the boats so they would intercept the convoy during the daylight hours to minimize the chance of its slipping through undetected in the dark. The boats were positioned too far apart to see each other, but close enough so the convoy could not pass between them without being seen.

Should the convoy not be sighted soon after the expected time, the BdU would re-deploy the group to find it. Sometimes it was necessary for him to spread his net of U-boats four or five times before making a catch, and success depended upon absolute accuracy in the form of navigation and position reports on the part of the boats, since even a slight error would leave a gap large enough for the convoy to slip through.

It was an effective system for Dönitz's highly trained and thoroughly disciplined grey wolves, who could hunt for days with such precision and teamwork, and then fight like demons for several more when the convoy was located.

The commander might well be dead on his feet from lack of sleep, and his crew as frazzled as himself, but exhausted minds and bodies had to work at top efficiency if a wolf pack were to fight effectively. It was this remarkable stamina and capacity for endurance under absolutely any conditions that made the German wolf packs the terror of the convoy lanes.

When a boat made contact with a convoy, her

commander was not allowed to attack immediately, but must first notify headquarters, giving the position, speed, and course of the convoy. This report, in case it had not already been picked up by the other boats in the group, was then signaled to them, and all of them set their courses to intercept.

The boat making initial contact had to keep shadowing the convoy, staying on the surface and out of sight, reporting all changes, but not attacking until at least one other boat reported contact. This insured that all the boats should be able to find the convoy, preferably before the first attack was launched. In the event that the first boat to attack might be driven deep and so lose contact, there would always be at least one boat to give the position and guide the others in. This was especially important if the convoy altered course after the first attack.

Once the signal to attack was given, all control from headquarters ceased and each commander was on his own. His only concern with the other boats in the group was to avoid colliding with them.

A group might thus haunt a convoy for days, shadowing and exchanging signals with each other by day, and returning with the darkness to rip the night apart with the ferocity of a wolf pack attack.

This, in brief, was the famous "Rudel-taktik" developed by Dönitz and brilliantly carried out by the handful of men he had so meticulously trained. Their success was phenomenal.

In the convoy battle that came to be known as the "Night of the Long Knives," the 34-ship convoy, SC 7, homeward bound from Nova Scotia, was intercepted northwest of Rockall Bank, some 250 miles from Ireland. Initial contact had been made by U-48 (Korvettenkapitän Bleichrodt) on the night of October 16-17,

1940, but he lost contact when he was attacked with depth charges by one of the escorts.

Dönitz then ordered the other boats in the group into a line across the presumed course of the convoy, and contact was regained on the afternoon of October 19. The pack of seven boats closed in and attacked soon after dark, sinking 17 ships during the night.

The following night, five boats sank 14 ships out of Convoy HX 79, and then met Convoy HX 79A, sinking seven more merchantmen. In all, the eight German U-boats that delivered these surfaced night attacks sank 38 ships out of three different convoys in a three-day battle. Not a U-boat was lost.

From the beginning, when Dönitz was ordered to build and command a U-boat arm for the German Navy, he had forseen that in any future war, Germany would fight against England. And he knew that as long as Britain ruled the waves, she could not be beaten. He recognized the U-boat as the one weapon that could give Germany the means to deny Britain control of the seas, and he set 300 operational boats as the absolute minimum with which to begin a war against Britain. With this number, he could have 100 boats in their operational areas at all times, allowing one third of the total to be in ports and dockyards, and a further third on their way to and from their operational areas.

When war broke out, he had exactly 57 boats, 46 of which were operational. And of these, only 22 were the Type VII or Type IX ocean-going boats, the rest being the "Einbäume," coastal boats of 250 tons.

Twenty-eight boats were lost during the first year, and 28 more commissioned, leaving the total number the same. But Germany began the second year of the war with only 27 boats available for operations, since some were on shakedown cruises, and it was necessary to hold back some of the available boats for training purposes.

During the war, a total of 863 German U-boats became operational. Seven hundred fifty-three were sunk, with the overwhelming loss of 32,000 officers and men out of a total strength of 39,000. They sank 148 Allied warships and damaged a further 45, and destroyed a total of 2,759 merchantmen with an aggregate of 14,119,413 gross register tons.[1]

Although the U-boat branch began the war woefully short of numbers, the weapon they had was excellent, and the men were superbly trained.

With the establishment of bases on the Bay of Biscay, the U-boats hit their stride and the first "Golden Age" was launched. The British, alarmed at their mounting losses, began sending most of their ships in convoys now, and the U-boats attacked them with skill, determination and ferocity, both in packs and alone.

Along with U-95, Schulz took his boat out from Lorient on her third war cruise on December 16. Her operational area was to be west of the Hebrides in the North Atlantic, and this time she was to be part of a wolf pack.

By the time she reached her station, she had come into the full fury of the storms that would rage for weeks on end and make this winter the worst in years. Plans for fighting as a group were abandoned in the face of the fierce storms and the boats were turned loose to hunt as best they could alone.

There had been another change in the wardroom

---

1. Gross register tonnage is the measure in hundreds of cubic feet of the enclosed spaces in the ship. Light displacement tonnage is the weight of the ship alone, and loaded displacement tonnage is the weight of the ship plus stores, water, fuel, etc., and capacity cargo.

on this trip. Hein Hirsacker had been relieved as I. WO by the radiant and brilliant Jochen Mohr. Young and irrepressibly gay, Mohr had already proved himself an extraordinarily gifted officer. During the Spanish Civil War in 1936, he had at the age of 19 carried out a highly successful secret mission when he was sent in civilian clothes from the battleship DEUTSCHLAND to spirit a group of German diplomats out of Tenerife.

Soon after this, when a similar mission was contemplated, Mohr was deemed the logical choice for it, and a request was forwarded to the DEUTSCHLAND's captain asking for his release. The request was answered with a curt refusal: *"Nein, der Mohr hat nicht seiner Schuldigkeit getan."* (Mohr has not finished his duties.) It was a message Mohr would meet again, in slightly different form, under vastly different circumstances.

He had served as flag lieutenant under Admiral Marschall on both the battleships SCHARNHORST and GNEISENAU until 1940, when he went to Norway to U-boat school. From then on, Mohr was a submariner, heart and soul. A born leader, he seemed to possess every special quality called for in a U-boat officer, and from the moment he set foot on board U-124, his life was inextricably bound to hers.

The U-124 men were used to the discomforts provided by a U-boat in the wintry North Atlantic. Without a heating or air-conditioning system, the temperature inside the boat was roughly that of the water outside. The running diesels did not noticeably warm the boat in cold waters, although in the tropics they combined with the merciless sun pounding down on the steel hull to shoot the temperature up past 140 degrees.

The eternally soggy air inside kept everything

green with mold, and imparted its share to the distinctive smell of a U-boat, a malevolent odor compounded in part of cooking smells, diesel oil, sweaty bodies, bilges, the infamous Tube 7, and a gagging dash of "colibri," the wicked-smelling cologne the men used to wash the salt spray off their hands and faces.

These things were daily annoyances they had learned to cope with by alternately ignoring them or joking about them. Now with heavy seas and freezing gale winds, life became unbearable aboard the U-boat. She rolled and pitched like a wild thing so that the men had to hold on constantly to keep from being flung willy-nilly about the boat. It was impossible to cook regular meals, and they ate their cold sandwiches with one hand while they held on with the other.

Visibility was so poor that reconnaissance was all but impossible. Thirty-foot waves and winds reaching Force 7 kept visibility down to less than five miles during the seven to eight hours of daylight, and absolutely nil during the dark.

And as the days dragged into weeks without even a chance to fire a torpedo, the weariness and strain began to leave its mark on all of them. Bitter cold gales lashed the men on bridge watch with stinging sprays of icy salt water, and frequently whole waves would wash over the conning tower. The men were kept from being swept overboard only by the safety belts which fastened them to the bridge. And when their watch was finally over and they stumbled below, half-frozen and spent, all they had seen was the relentless North Atlantic storm.

Even during their watch-free hours, rest was impossible on the tossing, plunging boat as she swung like a demented pendulum. It was difficult to wedge oneself into a bunk securely enough to doze off, and

once asleep, if a man's muscles ever completely relaxed, he was promptly slammed either into the bulk-
head or onto the deck. In spite of heavy guard rails
on the bunks, sleeping men were tossed out of them,
even sometimes thrown out of a top bunk on one side
to land in the bottom bunk on the opposite side

Nerves and tempers were frayed beyond endurance as they battled against the savage seas and the
aching weariness that numbed their bodies and spirits. Ordinary conversations among close friends suddenly erupted into violent and bitter quarrels, and
they would be pulled apart just before the fists began
to fly. They would then retire muttering to their own
bunks, to lie facing the clammy steel walls cursing
dispiritedly.

Normally considerate and friendly officers and petty officers snapped at each other and at their men
and grew more edgy with each endless day that
passed. The jokes and wit that had always laced
every situation on board disappeared altogether and
no laughter echoed through the boat as each man
bent all his efforts to simply getting through each
moment as it came. Even the sunny Jochen Mohr
grew silent, his high spirits finally cut down by the
brutal storms that turned a happy boat into a steel
purgatory.

The commander held his crew together with his
own stamina and iron self-discipline. He appeared to
regard the relentless fury of the storm as an irritating
but unavoidable nuisance, no more. He carried out his
daily routine, both in the boat and on the bridge,
sharply and competently, and forced everyone else to
do the same. His superb bearing was a constant example to them all and his unshaken morale bolstered
theirs.

Only once did Kesselheim, who in addition to his

regular duties served as the commander's batman, see him with his guard down. He had entered Schulz's cabin to find him sitting on the edge of his bunk, shoulders drooping and head bowed, his hands over his face. When Kesselheim spoke to him, Schulz looked up, all the strain and exhaustion and despair of these hellish weeks at sea plainly written on his face.

He had succeeded so well in masking his own feelings that until this moment, it had never occurred to Kesselheim that the commander had been really affected by the pressures of this patrol.

Now he knew with startling clarity that it was the commander who had borne the brunt of all their misery, and for an unforgettable instant the 20-year-old boy glimpsed something of the weight and loneliness of command and the strength of the man who carried it.

No one knew better than Schulz the exhaustion and frustration of his crew, and he prayed for a ship to come along. Even one small victory would pep them up he thought, and give them a reason for what they had to endure. It would be unbearably cruel to bring them home without having sunk a single ship to compensate for it. But he knew that under these impossible conditions only blind luck could bring about even sighting, to say nothing of sinking, a ship.

On Christmas Eve, the hydrophone operator heard the sound of screws approaching, then receding. They hunted desperately, fighting their way through the heavy waves, searching for the ship they had heard. They found nothing.

It was a dismal Christmas for the men of the U-124. The pathetic little Christmas tree they had made and lovingly decorated with home-made ornaments did little to dispel the gloom, and in fact only served to remind the men of happier Christmases at home with their loved ones in a world that was not always wet and cold.

At this particular time, there were only three German U-boats at sea. Admiral Dönitz would later bitterly complain that the "war against England, the mighty sea power and our principal adversary, was being waged by from 120 to 240 men of the German U-boat arm."[1]

On January 6, Schulz's pious prayer was answered when he sighted the British freighter EMPIRE THUNDER. The 6,000-ton ship was perplexingly difficult target as she pounded through waves as high as a house. Schulz made his calculations quickly and precisely. He knew that in the storm he might get only one shot and it had to be good.

The torpedoes were set, and he chose the exact instant to fire.

The first shot missed, and Schulz quickly fired another. It also missed, and the U-boat clung fiercely to the freighter, determined not to lose contact.

Schulz brought her back into firing position and squinting through the periscope, fired again. The torpedo hit the freighter's bow and she stopped. Schulz took aim and fired again, but the torpedo proved faulty, and to his horror, turned in a circle to head back to the U-boat. It sped within a few meters of the boat, then vanished. Unnerved by this maverick fish, the commander fired a last shot.

"By God, hit!" he whispered as the torpedo left the tube.

It hit aft, and the plucky freighter went down by the stern. Schulz watched, his face impassive. What-

---

1. Dönitz, Adm. Karl. TEN YEARS & TWENTY DAYS, World Publishing Co., Cleveland and New York.

ever happened now, at least he would not bring his crew home scoreless.

A few days later he was sure he was close upon a convoy, but was unable to track it down in the storm. He had found himself within a couple of thousand meters of a British destroyer, but the mountainous waves made it impossible to attack. The destroyer was tossing as wildly as the U-boat and could not bring her guns to bear. And so the two enemies could only stare curiously at each other while they fought their common foe, the wintry North Atlantic. The seas that battered them so mercilessly had, for the moment, made them safe from each other.

U-124 returned to Lorient along with U-38 and U-96 on January 22, 1941, after the most exhausting and frustrating six weeks her crew had ever known.

Admiral Dönitz met them at the pier, shocked by the transformation in the fresh and confident crew he had seen off only six weeks earlier. His heart went out to these thin, tired sailors, standing at stiff attention to greet him. Their faces, etched with deep lines of fatigue, and the alarming loss of weight they had all suffered—as much as 20 and 30 pounds per man— spoke only too eloquently of the strain and weariness and disappointment they had endured.

These men were his own—these, and the others who manned the handful of U-boats under his command. He had personally trained them, and he knew all of the officers and most of the men.

This coldly formal genius, whose men called him the "Big Lion," regarded his grey wolves with warm affection, and was constantly concerned for their welfare. When at all possible, he was on the quay waiting when a boat returned from the front. He would greet the whole crew, and then have a short visit in the wardroom with the commander and his officers, at which time he would get a quick résumé of the cruise and any problems which might require prompt attention.

Later, after the commander had a chance to rest, he would bring his war diary to the admiral's office for a line-by-line examination. And woe to the unlucky commander who did not have a good explanation for any entry that hinted at a lack of aggressiveness.

It was generally agreed among U-boat skippers that it was better to tangle with a British destroyer than an angry Dönitz, and a dressing down from the admiral would leave a bold and clever U-boat commander feeling like a spanked puppy. More than one skipper, head held high and cheeks aflame, his decorations for gallantry gleaming against his freshly pressed uniform, would march from this office wondering dully how such a witless spineless dummkopf as himself could ever have been entrusted with command of a German U-boat in the first place. It would be hours later, over beer or wine with his fellow commanders before his confidence would return.

"God," sighed one after relating his conversation with the BdU, "I'd rather have a *real* lion get hold of me!"

Constant peak performance was expected by the admiral, and he would tolerate nothing less. His impossibly high standards, and their own ability to meet those standards month after month, in good times and bad, contributed to the intense pride and confidence of the U-boat men.

Their morale would soar in the months and years when, in spite of their absurdly small numbers, the German U-boat was the dread of the ocean, threatening every Allied ship that put to sea and wiping out whole convoys at a time. And it would remain unbroken in the face of devastating losses, during the last bitter months when only two out of every five U-boats that left on patrol would ever return.

Always behind them stood the Big Lion, demanding all they had to give in courage, endurance, and fighting skill, but fiercely protective whenever his cubs were threatened by an outsider, be it British warship or German brass.

Chapter Six

BEFORE LEAVING on his fourth war patrol in U-124, Schulz was called in for the usual briefing by Admiral Dönitz. The admiral informed him that in view of the short but successful cruise by U-65 around Freetown, during which she sank eight ships and damaged another, three other boats would be sent to this area. U-105 (Shewe), U-106 (Hermann Rasch), and U-124 (Schulz) would leave at two-day intervals. Since lack of fuel had cut short U-65's cruise, arrangements would be made to refuel and resupply these three boats at sea.

"Schulz, do you think you could get in and out of the harbor at Las Palmas at night without being seen?" the admiral asked suddenly.

Schulz considered for a moment, then replied that he was reasonably sure he could because he knew the harbor from his days on merchant ships.

"Good," the admiral said. "You will go in and refuel from a German tanker that is anchored in the harbor. She is the CORRIENTES, lying approximately here." He indicated the position on a chart of the harbor.

"But I must impress upon you, Schulz, that secrecy is of the utmost importance. You must not be seen."

If it became known that the tanker was supplying German U-boats, she would be forced to leave the neutral port. But if the refueling were successful, it would be a tremendous advantage to the Freetown boats to be able to top off their fuel tanks in the Canary Islands, well over half way to their operational area.

Just before Schulz left, the admiral handed him a small package, about the size and shape of a cigar box. "You are to give this to Kapitän Krancke, commander of the ADMIRAL SCHEER," he said. "A rendezvous will be arranged at sea. It is of vital importance to the SCHEER—and top secret."

Schultz took the package, wondering to himself what it could possibly contain that was so important to a pocket battleship.

"Goodbye," the admiral said, shaking hands with him warmly. "Good hunting."

U-124 arrived at Las Palmas about dark on March 4, and crept in close on the surface to observe. She spent the night lying just outside the harbor entrance while her commander watched the traffic that came and went, and timed the trips of the sentry pacing back and forth on the mole.

Just before daylight, Schulz brought his boat back out from the harbor and took her down to 50 meters. He then worked out his plans for the following night.

The men spent the day sleeping and resting, with only a skeleton crew on watch. There would be no sleep for anyone the next night.

It was quite dark when the boat came back to Las Palmas and waited while the sentry walked toward them on the mole. Then he started back in the opposite direction. As soon as his back was turned, U-124 crept stealthily into the narrow harbor entrance. She was flooded down so that the decks were awash and only the small conning tower was above the water. There were only three men on the bridge. Schulz and Mohr were observing forward while a petty officer watched aft.

They headed cautiously toward where Schulz had been told he would find the tanker. She would be lying at anchor inside the harbor but not at a pier, and Dönitz had given Schulz a silhouette of her for identification. They found her almost immediately and with no difficulties, picking her out from several other ships lying at anchor in the vicinity.

U-124 slipped warily alongside the tanker about 1 A.M. Immediately there was a great deal of subdued activity aboard the CORRIENTES as the U-boat tied up and Schulz and about half his crew went on board.

He was told the tanker had been notified by the German embassy in Spain to be on the lookout for a German U-boat which would refuel from them. They had been watching for two weeks, and although four men had been looking for the boat as she approached, none had seen her until she was within a few meters of the ship. This further convinced Schulz that a U-boat, riding low in the water at night, was all but invisible to a surface ship.

All the U-boat's crew went aboard the tanker to be treated to a good hot breakfast and a warm welcome from their countrymen while the boat took on diesel fuel, lubricating oil, drinking water, and other provisions. By 4 A.M., the refueling was finished and the U-boat again slipped through the harbor entrance just before daylight. The operation had been an unqualified success.

Shortly after clearing the harbor, the U-boat sighted a steamer, probably French or Portuguese, but Schulz let her go without a chase because they were too close to land.

The next night, March 5, they again made contact with another ship. They were running on the surface, and the balmy tropical night gave the illusion of a peacetime cruise to the men topside. Schulz had stayed on the bridge until nearly midnight, then had gone down to his bunk. He had just dropped off to sleep when the call, "Commander to the bridge!" sent him running topside.

This preemptory order roused many a weary skip-per from a sound sleep, groggy and swearing, and trying desperately to clear his sleep-drugged brain before he reached the bridge. Within seconds he must be able to make decisions for attacking, assess sudden danger that might be present, or cope with whatever situation had been deemed serious enough by the officer on watch to summon the commander. By the time he reached the bridge, he had to be alert enough to use all his skill, training and experience.

The new II.WO, Werner Henke, had the bridge watch. Catching a glimpse of white, he turned around as Schulz popped through the hatch. On a U-boat, only the commander wore a white hat, making him easy to recognize on a dark bridge.

Henke pointed out the two silhouettes some 6,000 meters distant. They were warships. Schulz closed in a little, and in a few minutes, he could tell they were either battleships or heavy cruisers.

Word had soon flashed through the boat that they were stalking two battleships, and though no orders had been given, the crew had quietly begun to close up to battle stations. Mohr had come onto the bridge.

While Schulz was maneuvering the boat into at-tacking position, he was full of doubts about the ships ahead. It seemed highly unlikely that two British heavy units would be in these waters without a destroyer screen. (God knows they had plenty of them, he thought to himself.) At least they should be zigzagging at high speed, but these two were proceeding on a straight course at about 7 knots.

"But if they were ours, we should have been told," he remarked perplexedly. "Check again, Mohr. And what would *ours* be doing cruising along like this in 'Britain's Ocean'?"

Mohr thumbed rapidly through the radio log and also asked Dr. Hubertus Goder, who in addition to his few duties as physician was part-time communications officer.

As a doctor, Goder was classified as a noncombatant, and so could not take part in such aggressive duties as standing a watch. Communications, being somehow considered more peaceful, was permissible, and Dr. Goder helped out by decoding messages which could be handled only by an officer. He told Mohr he had positively decoded no such message.

Within a few minutes Mohr was back on the bridge to report to the commander that no signal had been received regarding German warships in the area.

Schulz hesitated. He did not believe that British battleships would be out without a strong destroyer escort. Still, the SKL (Seekriegsleitung—Naval High Command) would surely have informed him if German ships were in the vicinity.

The officers on the bridge stared intently at the dark ships, growing steadily larger as the distance closed. The situation was as puzzling as ever to Schulz. If they were, indeed, British, it was a U-boat commander's dream come true. But if they were German, then he stood to claim the nightmarish distinction of striking a crippling blow against his own navy and slaughtering several thousand of his countrymen.

"Mohr," he said finally, "get a message off to the BdU and ask if any German heavy units could be in our area."

"In the meantime," he went on as Mohr disappeared down the conning tower hatch, "we'll circle around ahead and be in position to shoot. By the time we get ready to fire, we should have an answer."

Inside the boat, the impatient men waited at their battle stations. "Why doesn't he shoot? What's he waiting for?" "They're bound to be British. They'd have told us if our own ships were out here." "Keep your shirt on. Willem knows what he's doing. If they're British, he'll sink them."

And on the bridge, "Willem" stared at the unsuspecting warships moving serenely on their way and hoped desperately that he was not letting a perfect shot at two capital ships slip through his fingers.

Suddenly the two ships lurched to high speed and began zig-zagging wildly.

"We've lost them now," the disappointed murmur went across the narrow bridge.

But Schulz laughed aloud. "They're German all right. And I'll guarantee they just got word a U-boat was after them!"

"Wait, Herr Kaleu!" Goder yelled, scrambling onto the bridge waving the wireless message Chief Radioman Schroeder had handed him and which he had just decoded: *"Es ist mit auftreten eigener schwerer Streitkräfte in ihrem aufmarsch Gebiet zu rechnen."* (It is to be reckoned with own heavy units appearing in your operational area.)

When Schulz's signal arrived at U-boat Headquarters, Dönitz had called up the Naval Commander/

West, announced that one of his U-boats was getting ready to torpedo two unescorted battleships, and gave him the position.

"My God!" shrieked the Commander/West. "That's SCHARNHORST and GNEISENAU!"

"Thank you," replied Dönitz, and hung up. He later tartly suggested to the Commander/West that he be kept informed of the whereabouts of German battleships in the future.

The frantic warning from the Commander/West reached the two battleships only a minute ahead of the BdU's signal to Schulz. And a cold shudder ran over the officers in the Naval Headquarters when they thought of the unspeakable disaster so narrowly averted. Thank God Schulz had been suspicious of the ships and had not been too trigger-happy to call up for verification.

Next afternoon, U-124's path again crossed that of the GNEISENAU. This time it was daylight, and there was no difficulty in recognizing her.

Schulz closed in until he was near enough for her to see him. Then, having no wish for his own boat to be the victim of mistaken identity, he turned to lie broadside to the battleship. In this position, neither his bow nor stern tubes could be brought to bear. GNEISENAU approached cautiously, her guns trained on the U-boat.

As she came alongside U-124, Admiral Lütjens hailed the boat and asked if she were the one that had shadowed them the night before.

Schulz replied that she was. His answer caused a visible stir on board the huge battleship as men crowded the rails to stare curiously at the U-boat, the edelweiss on her conning tower brilliant in the sunlight.

"Tell me," Lütjens asked Schulz, "could you have torpedoed us?"

A sudden silence fell over them as the men strained forward to hear the answer.

"Easily!"

The admiral stared thoughtfully at the confident and self-possessed U-boat commander below him. "Then I thank you for saving my life," he said, a faint smile touching his lips.

On March 8, U-124 had yet another contact with SCHARNHORST and GNEISNAU, when the battleships located the British Convoy SL 67, escorted by the battleship MALAYA. The German ships were under orders not to attack convoys which contained heavy units, so they had fallen back and called up U-124 and U-105, both of which were in the vicinity, giving them the position of the convoy.

Schulz raced toward the convoy at full speed, trying to cover as much distance as possible before dark. He reached his estimated point of interception shortly after dark, but there was no sign of the convoy.

Frowning, he climbed down into the control room to go over his plots at the chart table. Deciding correctly that he had crossed the convoy's course behind the ships, he set a new course.

Again they passed the interception point without sighting the convoy, and Schulz wondered anxiously if they had missed it altogether. He rechecked his plots, and decided this time they must have crossed ahead of the convoy. While he was still going over his figures, an excited shout from above electrified everyone in the control room.

"Commander to the bridge!"

Schulz dropped his pencil and ran up the ladder. He was on the bridge almost before the sentence was finished.

"Look, Herr Kaleu," Mohr pointed. "The battleship!"

"Make ready all torpedo tubes!" the commander called. "Prepare for surfaced torpedo attack! Come to course one-three-o!"

The U-boat had scarcely settled on her new course when the battleship turned. "Hard port!" Schulz said. Then he leaned over the open hatch. "Commander to L.I.!"

Brinker's upturned face appeared below him.

"I've got to have more speed, Brinker," Schulz told him.

"This is all she'll do, Herr Kaleu," Brinker called back. "She's wide open now."

"Well it's not good enough!" Schulz shouted impatiently. "Have a talk with those diesels. This is a battleship we're after, and she's fast as the devil!"

"Aye, sir. Will do."

Brinker turned and went back into the engine room. "Boys," he yelled above the noise of the diesels, "there's a fast lady up there, and the commander says he's got to have more speed to catch her! Let's see what we can give him!"

"Aye, Herr Brinker!" the men nodded, grinning. This was the sort of challenge they liked. Somehow they would give Willem the speed he asked for.

"Commander to control room!"

"Control room here!"

"Be ready to shoot as soon as I give the settings. It will have to be a quick shot. She's wild as an ape!"

The U-boat turned back and forth in an effort to close in on the erratically zig-zagging battleship and get in a position to attack. She was steaming fast, with such rapid and unpredictable turns that Schulz was finding it difficult even to maintain contact with her in the pitch black night.

"Well, Henke," he said casually to the II.WO, "have you got her zig-zag pattern figured yet?"

"Good Lord, no!" answered Henke. "I think they're making it up as they go along!"

"I think whoever's got the conn is drunk," Mohr announced. "Somebody's been spiking the Tommies' tea!"

Schulz and Henke laughed. "Well, one thing is sure," Schulz said. "Drunk or sober, that old girl knows all about U-boats, and I'm not going to waste any more time with her. We'll go find the children instead of waltzing in the dark with Mamma all night. That convoy's close."

The U-boat turned, searching the blackness around them for some sign of the merchant ships that had thus far eluded them.

"Ship in sight!"

Schulz turned to watch the sleek destroyer gliding up on their starboard quarter. She was not heading directly for them.

"Port fifteen!" he called. "Come to 265 degrees."

"Port fifteen. Come to 265 degrees." The order was repeated below to Kundt, the helmsman, who acknowledged. A second later, the boat heeled over gently with the turn.

"That should be the sweeper," Schulz remarked to Mohr, meaning the escort that ranged back and forth in front of the convoy. "And now for the convoy!"

The long hunt was finally over as U-124 steamed calmly on the surface into the midst of the merchant ships. They were ranged in staggered columns, about 800 meters apart, and they moved steadily through the long swells, unaware of the U-boat that had turned around and was now traveling along with them.

With Mohr as torpedo officer, Schulz had quickly

set up an attack in the almost overwhelming abundance of targets that now surrounded him. Only a few seconds remained before the torpedoes would be fired when a brilliant flash lit up the port side of the convoy, followed by the rumbling roar of the explosion. U-105 had torpedoed an auxiliary cruiser, which burst into flames. Schewe had beat them to the punch!

The hated star shells were now fired from every direction, lighting up the convoy with dazzling brilliance. The men on U-124's bridge stared apprehensively at the merchant ships towering around them. Seconds before, they had been only vague hulking shapes in the black night. Now they were lit up as brightly as in a peacetime port, and one of them was well under the minimum distance of 300 meters required for firing a torpedo.

Schulz watched the men lining the rails of the freighter on his starboard side. He could see the glowing lights reflected on their faces as they watched the burning ship. How could they keep from seeing the U-boat so close beside them, he wondered frantically, and won't those damned star shells ever go out?

Still the Britishers stared at the hypnotic red flames that marked the loss of one of their ships and the death of seamen like themselves, and never once did they glance down at their deadly little companion, steaming along unnoticed beside them. Perhaps the last place they would have expected to see a U-boat was where U-124 was: on the surface squarely in the middle of a British convoy.

At last the star shells went out, and the night was infinitely blacker after their blinding glare. It was time for U-124 to try her luck.

"Here, Mohr," Schulz said, pointing. "This target."

Mohr bent over the night sight, making rapid calculations. Schulz quickly chose targets as he put his boat in position to attack. They would fire as many torpedoes as possible at as many different targets, and an attack like this had to be fast and exact. Once the first torpedo hit, the confused movements of the other ships could ruin the other shots.

"Wait, Herr Kaleu!" Mohr suddenly cried. "See? This one is bigger!" He motioned to another ship close to their first target.

"Okay," answered Schulz. "Take her."

It was the same with the next. "Herr Kommandant, this one is bigger!" Mohr was wild with excitement. "Wait! Here's one even bigger!"

"For God's sake, Mohr," Schulz screamed, "shoot!"

Grins appeared on the bridge watch's faces, and Mohr leaned over the night sight as he industriously called out the torpedo settings.

The torpedoes left the tubes at rapid intervals. Four from the bow tubes, two from the stern, all aimed at different targets.

The first torpedo hit a freighter of about 9,000 tons from a distance of 1500 meters. They saw her sink immediately. The second hit a 6,000-ton ship 900 meters away, setting her afire. Another 6,000-ton freighter, some 2,000 meters away, caught the third torpedo. She also burned, and they watched her sinking, her bow under water up to her running lights.

The fourth torpedo was a stern shot, and hit a 7,000-ton freighter from a distance of 700 meters. The look-outs saw her sink. The fifth shot, also from a stern tube, hit a 5,000-ton freighter 1500 meters away. The lookouts could see she was going down by the stern, up to the main deck in water, presumed sinking.

Schulz watched the track of his sixth torpedo, shot from a bow tube, as it sped toward a large freighter on his port quarter. It was running straight and true, leading the ship enough to meet her precisely amidships.

Suddenly he noticed a turbulence in the ship's wake and remarked to Mohr, "We'll miss this one. Her captain's seen the torpedo track and ordered her full astern."

As the ship abruptly slowed her speed, the torpedo with her name on it sped harmlessly across her bow, only a few meters away. The freighter master's order had saved his ship.

U-124's position was now clearly marked by the torpedo tracks running out like the spokes on a wheel, and a destroyer was racing directly for them.

"Alarm!" yelled Schulz. "Dive! Dive!"

As the boat dived, they knew they could expect no depth charges in the middle of these merchant ships. Their tubes were empty, and in an attack lasting less than 10 minutes, they had counted four ships sunk. The torpedo that passed ahead of its target went on to find another, however, and the count was actually five ships.

U-124's crew congratulated themselves on their success. Not a bad bag for ten minutes work! Their Willem had certainly blitzkrieged this convoy. The destroyer up there knew where they were, but there was nothing she could do about it. Besides, she would have her hands full picking up her own survivors. Meantime, they would reload their torpedo tubes and come back to have another crack at the convoy.

Then through the hull of the U-boat came noises from the water around them—the chilling and unmistakable sound of ships breaking up as they sank. The U-boat men looked at each other, the triumph drained from tense frightened faces. Suppose one of those torpedoed ships came down on top of them?

How macabre to be carried to the bottom by one's own victim!

To watch a ship sink from the surface was a tragic sight, no matter how hard one had worked to bring about just that event. But to be under water, and to hear the sounds from within a dying ship was a horribly graphic preview of what the U-124's crew knew perfectly well could happen to them at any time. The rending crumpling sound of bulkheads caved in by the water pressure made their flesh crawl, and they stared at their own grey bulkheads. Would these same awful sounds be someday repeated in their own boat, and would these sturdy steel walls be crumpled around them for a torn and jagged coffin?

Schulz looked up and shuddered involuntarily. Was one of those sinking ships above them? As terrifying as the depth charges were, this was worse. How grisly to be locked in a fatal embrace with a wrecked ship, to be caught and crushed and borne down to the bottom of the ocean by a ship he himself had torpedoed. It was like being carried to one's death by a corpse. He shuddered again and bit his lip.

At last they were free of the carnage around them, and they reloaded the torpedo tubes and surfaced, forcing themselves to shake off the clammy fear that had gripped them. In the distance, lights flickered as rescue boats moved slowly through the water picking up survivors.

Now rearmed, U-124 started after the convoy again, but was forced under by a destroyer which dropped a few depth charges, none very close. And while the destroyer kept the U-Boat down, the mangled convoy made its escape.

Next morning, Schulz again made contact with SCHARNHORST, but the battleship could offer no clue to the convoy's position. Schulz was sure it had altered course, but could find no trace of it.

Still hunting, he met U-106 and talked to her commander, but Rasch was also at a loss as to the convoy's whereabouts.

Unable to relocate the ships, Schulz resumed his interrupted journey toward the West African coast. The cruise had begun with striking success.

A few days after the convoy battle, Dr. Goder was called in to see Maschinistmaat Toni Walbröl, who was lying in his bunk, feverish from a painfully infected arm. For several days, Dr. Goder treated it, but the injury had been severe and the infection was seriously advanced, so that in spite of all the doctor could do, Walbröl grew steadily worse.

Finally Goder told the commander that an operation was imperative—an operation that would be impossible to perform on the U-124.

"Why wasn't I told about it when he got hurt?" Schulz demanded irritably. "His arm was already badly infected before I even heard about it."

"It happened in port, Herr Kaleu," Goder told him. "A couple of days before we left Lorient."

"Well why didn't he get it taken care of then instead of letting it get in this shape?" Schulz asked, surprised to find that the injury had occurred some two weeks before. "He could have gone to a hospital then."

"That's what he was afraid of," Goder said. "He didn't tell anybody because he was afraid he'd be put in a hospital and the boat would sail without him."

Walbröl was one of the original crew that had survived the sinking of the U-64.

Schulz shook his head. "That was very foolish," he said. "It was dangerous for him; and besides, I need every man I have. I certainly ought not to leave base with any casualties on board."

"I agree absolutely, Herr Kommandant," Goder said innocently. "But I wonder what you would have done under the circumstances."

"That's entirely beside the point, Doctor," Schulz snapped. But his brown eyes flickered in sudden amusement as he conjured up the preposterous mental picture of his sitting tamely by with a bandaged arm while some other commander took his boat on patrol. "You've made your point, Doctor," he said, grinning. "I'm going to see Walbröl now. And if you can put off surgery for two more days, I'll have a real operating theatre for you. We rendezvous with the KORMORAN on the 18th."

The rendezvous point was south of Freetown out in the open Atlantic. U-124 arrived at the precise spot at the precise moment in a raging storm—and with her officers and crew understandably congratulating themselves on a fine piece of seamanship. Taking on torpedoes was impossible in the weather, a fact that was rather forcefully brought home to both commanders when the attempt resulted in damaging the one torpedo that survived the precarious trip. They then agreed on a second rendezvous and met there a few hours later.

The weather was still too rough for the U-boat to be supplied, but Dr. Goder and Walbröl were taken over to the auxiliary cruiser in a small boat. Goder, assisted by the KORMORAN's surgeon, operated as soon as they arrived.

The storm was worse when he finished, so he was obliged to remain on board the KORMORAN until the next day, and spent his time basking in the luxurious wardroom and officers' quarters on the raider. As soon as his duties in surgery were completed, he plunged enthusiastically into his role as man of the hour, every inch the dashing U-boat officer as he told his fascinated audience about their encounters with the SCHORNHORST and GNEISENAU and the convoy battle that followed.

After waiting some four hours for the weather to improve, U-124 took on four torpedoes forward and two aft, and also a replacement for the injured Walbröl, Obermaschinistmaat Ackermann.

It was the following morning before the diesel oil and fresh water could be taken aboard, and with the completion of transfers all concerned breathed a sigh of relief. Rendezvous points were always chosen for their remoteness, but should an enemy plane or ship stumble upon one, the ships engaged in refueling would be helpless to fight or run.

Soon after the hoses were uncoupled, the tripod masts of a warship appeared on the horizon. Schulz had been notified that the pocket battleship ADMIRAL SCHEER would join them at the rendezvous, but he cautiously dived to take a good first look through the periscope. It was always possible that a Britisher had decided to crash the party, and it was healthy to be discreet in U-boat circles.

When the SCHEER hove to near the raider, U-124 surfaced and Schulz signaled to Kapitän Theodor Krancke that he had brought his cigar box. Krancke replied that he was sending a boat and also a surprise for U-124.

The boat arrived loaded with fresh-baked bread and cakes, a rare treat for the U-boat men whose rations mostly came out of cans—and even these tasted like diesel oil. Schulz, cigar box in hand, returned with the boat to the SCHEER, and handed it over to Krancke, who received it with joyous relief.

Later, while he was entertaining Schulz and Kap-

itän Detmars of the KORMORAN, he was informed
that Schulz's mysterious box had done the trick, and
at last Schulz learned its contents.

It was a replacement quartz for the SCHEER's
radar, which had been out of commission. The battleship was ready to try to break through the British
fleet to get home again, an almost hopeless task without her radar.

While the SCHEER's repaired radar scanned the
distance and her big guns loomed protectively over
them, the little German fleet lay together off St. Paul's
Rocks in the South Atlantic, and the crews eagerly
visited back and forth among the ships.

The U-124 men rapturously stretched their legs and
ate wonderful fresh foods on board the big ships. And
they reveled in the unaccustomed luxury of a bath.
The bountiful supply of fresh water even allowed for
laundry, so the scrubbed U-boat crew turned out in
clean uniforms too.

They noted with amusement that eager as the big
ship men were to visit their U-boat, they were all
even more eager to leave it, profoundly influenced by
claustrophobia and the special U-boat aroma which
the natives on board did not even notice any more.

They lounged lazily on the decks, dreamily
watching the flying fish that sailed through the air
around them. Some of the graceful little fish leaped
over the bow of the boat, and a few fell short to land
on the deck.

Kesselheim gathered up a batch of them, intending
to dry them like herring and take them home as a
souvenir of this cruise. The attempt was a spectacular
failure, however, and after a few days, the smell of
dead fish in the forward torpedo room was overpowering. Kesselheim received an ultimatum from his

shipmates telling him that if the fish were not thrown overboard immediately, he himself would be.

The ships' companies amused each other by demonstrating their special qualities and accomplishments. SCHEER, of course, awed the others with her heavy guns and armament, as well as her spanking Navy beauty and impressive size.

KORMORAN, Ship 41, was a former merchantman converted into an auxiliary cruiser, and she demonstrated how she could change herself within seconds from an innocent-looking freighter into a formidable raider, bristling with guns. This high-seas Houdini could and did approach enemy ships without arousing suspicion until she unmasked her guns and ordered them to stop. Her disguise was so perfect that even the most critical close inspection revealed absolutely no flaw, and the crews of the SCHEER and U-124 were fascinated.

U-124, determined not to be outdone, showed the others how fast a U-boat could dive, and vanished from the surface as though by magic.

Before the little fleet dispersed, the SCHEER bound for home, KORMORAN to the Pacific, and U-124 to the African coast, Kapitän Krancke asked Schulz what he could do for U-124. "Isn't there some special food you'd like to take aboard?"

"No, no," answered Schulz politely. "You'll need your own provisions, and we have plenty to last us." He tried to keep his mind off the delicious broiled steaks and fresh vegetables he and all his men had been served on board this floating palace.

"Then how about some nice fresh eggs?" Krancke asked.

"Oh, if you could spare us a few, we would like that very much," Schulz answered.

"Fine," said Krancke. "Now how many thousands do you think you can use?"

"*Thousands?*" gasped Schulz.

Krancke related, with obvious enjoyment, how the SCHEER had captured the refrigerator ship DUQUESA, which carried a cargo of 9,000 tons of meat and fruit and 900 tons of eggs. This sea-going delicatessen had then supplied all the German ships in the South Atlantic with goodies they never dreamed they would see until they got back to base.

U-124 left the rendezvous crammed, like the others, with fresh eggs. Her crew ate eggs morning, noon, and night to use them up before they spoiled—fried eggs, boiled eggs, scrambled eggs, omelets—until they, like the crews of all the other ships that shared in this bounty, were so thoroughly sick of eggs they never wanted to see another one.

On March 22, three days after leaving the rendezvous, U-124 was approaching the African coast when one of the diesel machinists came to Brinker with the ominous report, "No oil pressure in the starboard diesel."

Brinker hurried to the engine room and opened the side panels under the pistons. Oil was pouring out. Each diesel had nine pistons and 11 bearings, and in this engine, only two bearings were intact. Two were totally destroyed, and the rest partially destroyed.

Brinker shut off the engine, and reported to Schulz that the starboard diesel was out of order and could not be used at all until it was repaired. They would have to stop immediately.

Schulz made no effort to conceal his anger and disgust, but he clearly had no choice. He fretted and stewed on the bridge, anxiously watching for planes and ships while his boat lay dead in the water, a sitting duck.

"Ship on the starboard beam, sir," a lookout reported.

Schulz studied the tiny shadow on the horizon. Then he grabbed the speaking tube. "Kommandant to L.I.!" he said.

A few seconds later, Brinker's voice came up to him. "L.I. here."

"Brinker," Schulz told him, "I want all the speed I can get on the port diesel. I'm going after this ship."

"I'll do the best I can, Herr Kaleu," Brinker answered, turning away with a shrug.

Schulz worked for hours to bring his crippled boat into position to fire; but the ship, apparently a liner of the Highland class, had too much speed for him and escaped before he could get off a shot.

Again they lay stopped while the L.I. and his gang worked on the starboard diesel.

Finally Brinker's head appeared at the hatch. "Permission to come on the bridge?"

"Permission granted. Come on up." Schulz waited impatiently while Brinker climbed up. "Well, come on," he said. "Is the engine fixed yet?"

Brinker hesitated. Then he said slowly, "Herr Kommandant, the starboard engine is not fixed. And now the same thing has happened to the port engine. We can't use either one."

For a moment Schulz seemed stunned by the news. Then he said, "How long will it take to fix them?"

"They can't be fixed, Herr Kaleu," Brinker replied. "We'll have to scuttle the boat."

"We will certainly *not* scuttle my boat, L.I.!" Schulz snapped angrily. "We'll sit here til you fix those engines!"

"But Herr Kommandant," wailed Brinker, "there are eight bearings totally destroyed, to say nothing of the ones partially destroyed, and we have only four bearings in reserve. I don't have anything to make new ones out of, and without the diesels, we can't even recharge the batteries!"

"Don't you think I know that?" shouted Schulz. "And I also know this area is full of British planes and destroyers just looking for a nice fat target like us!"

Brinker started to reply, but was cut off by a torrent of words from his furious commander. "And you stand here telling me you don't have enough bearings! Well, *make* them! I don't give a damn how you do it, but fix those diesels and that's an order!"

He stopped, out of breath, and Brinker took advantage of the pause to beat a hasty retreat. He had merely informed the commander of the facts, and had not expected any such explosion on the part of the usually reasonable Schulz. He started back to the engine room, half his mind cursing the commander for a stubborn, obstinate, bull-headed Prussian, the other half casting about frantically for a solution to his apparently insoluble problem.

Certainly he could make the bearings, if he had the right kind of metal. But he didn't have it, and there was simply no way of getting it.

His men looked up anxiously as he stumbled swearing into the engine room.

"The Old Man says to fix the diesels," he announced. "We are to make new bearings."

"Out of *what*, Herr Brinker?" asked Dieselmaschinist Richter.

"Herr Kapitänleutnant Wilhelm Georg Schulz didn't tell me that," Brinker answered sarcastically. "Old socks, perhaps. Or we could send out to the nearest metal dealer and order what we want."

He thrust his hands belligerently into his pockets. Most any thin lightweight metal would do, one that could be shaped to the proper form. His fingers closed around the pack of cigarettes in his pocket.

Unfortunately, there was no such metal on board, and ten commanders yelling "that's an order" on the bridge wouldn't make any. He slid his fingers glumly around the top of the cigarette pack—sheets of thin metal—suddenly he snatched the pack out of his pocket and tore it open. The foil in the package—thin metal—it just might work, if they could get enough of it. It was worth a try.

Within minutes the machinists had collected the tin foil from every pack of cigarettes on board and set about turning it into replacement bearings for the diesels. Brinker sent word to the commander that they were making the bearings, but it would take time.

The commander coldly sent word back to Brinker that time was something they might not have much of and he had better hurry. Lying dead in the water so close to an enemy base made one a poor insurance risk, and visibility was appallingly good.

While the machinists worked feverishly and the commander nervously paced his bridge, expecting the entire British navy to descend on him at any moment, the off-duty sailors fatalistically ignored the whole situation. They watched the sharks circling around the boat, dispatching them with pistol shots whenever they came within range. Then they made a large hook, baited it with fat, and managed to land five blue sharks, some of them nine and ten feet long. With a sailor's dread of the brutes, they killed them and tossed them back in the ocean, saving only a few fins which they hung on the conning tower as trophies.

Ten hours after they had stopped, Brinker came to the bridge, a broad grin on his face.

"Permission to start engines, sir?"

"Granted, L.I.!" Schulz replied. "Are they all right?"

"I can't tell till we get started, sir," Brinker said. "But Herr Kommandant, they must be run very slowly at first to see if the bearings will hold."

After 14 anxious hours of slow running, Brinker tried them at full speed.

"Looks like they're OK, sir," he told the commander. "Running good as new."

"Thank God," Schulz murmured fervently. "And you might like to know, Brinker," he added casually, "that I'm recommending you for the Knight's Cross."

On March 30, about 200 miles west of Freetown, U-124 sighted a single-traveling freighter. It was an easy target for Schulz, and he moved into firing position for a submerged attack.

It was around noon, and as he made his shooting observation, he could see the cook in his tall white cap resting his arms on the rail. They must be eating lunch, Schulz thought. How peaceful she looked, and he could vividly picture the scene on board. And how different it would all be in a few minutes! But he was looking at it through the lens of an attack periscope, and he shook off these disquieting thoughts, thoughts not permitted in a U-boat commander.

"Torpedo . . . los!"

The torpedo hit, and threw the ship into wild confusion as men ran back and forth. A boat was launched, and it pulled away from the stricken ship.

Schulz waited a few minutes. "One fish isn't going to sink her," he said. "But we'll give them time to get off before we shoot again."

"Herr Kaleu," the radio man called, "ship is signalling on the 600 meter band." He handed Schulz

Wilhelm Schulz, commander of U-164 and first commander of U-124.

Commissioning ceremony aboard U-124 at Bremen, 11 June, 1940. Schulz at right on bridge, next to flag.

U-64 commissioned into service, 15 December, 1939.

Jochen Mohr, photographed on the bridge of U-124 by
Wilhelm Schulz.

In the early months aboard U-124, from left to right: Medical
Officer Hubertus Goder, 1st Watch Officer Jochen Mohr, 2nd
Watch Officer Werner Henke.

U-124 leaving the harbor at Lorient.

Survivors of the *Tweed* are rescued by crewmen of U-124. At left of Mohr (who is indicated by arrow) is Baker, 3rd Officer of the *Tweed*.

U-124 entering port in Lorient, 29 December, 1941, after sinking *Dunedin* and *Sagadahoc*.

Tanker *British Resource*, sunk off Cape Hatteras on 14 March, 1942.

Crewman of U-124 lends a hand to survivors of the *Umona*.

Kapitanleutnant Jochen Mohr called to the bridge of U-124 to celebrate his winning of the Knight's Cross with a party and (*below*) a "Knight's Cross Cake" presented by members of the crew.

U-124 cruising in the South Atlantic, 1943, and (*below*) looking aft at the wake of the U-124 . . . grey wolf, grey sea.

the signal he had copied: S O S S O S de g s d f UMONA 7 r 42 N, 14 r 40 W torpedoed.

Meantime, the men in the boat returned to their ship and came back aboard.

"What are they doing?" Schulz muttered, exasperated. "Don't they know that ship hasn't a prayer?" And he waited a little longer.

Twenty minutes after the first torpedo, he shot the second. The ship went down like a stone.

After watching her sink, Schulz ordered the boat down to 50 meters, and called the crew into the control room.

"Bring out the champagne," he said. "If my calculations are right, this ship brings my tonnage score up to 100,000 tons sunk, and I should get the Knight's Cross. Let's celebrate now!"

"Yes, Herr Kaleu," Brinker told him, coming into the control room. "You already have it! Uncle Karl[1] figures higher than you do. Congratulations!"

Kesselheim handed a wireless message to him. "This came during the attack, sir. I couldn't disturb you then. Congratulations!"

The beaming crew broke into cheers, and presented their commander with a Knight's Cross they had already made for him. It was hung around his neck with all due ceremony, and he wore it proudly and constantly. The cook brought in the cake he had baked, lavishly decorated with a Knight's Cross in icing, and they all drank a toast in champagne as they celebrated their success.

Four days later, U-124 again crossed the position where they had sunk the UMONA. They spotted one small raft with three men on it, and pulled alongside.

One of the men seemed to be unconscious, and the

---

1. Uncle Karl: nickname for Admiral Karl Dönitz.

other two in a state of shock. They told Schulz they were from the UMONA, the only survivors as far as they knew, and asked if he were the U-boat that had sunk them.

"Yes," replied Schulz. "But why, *why* didn't you abandon ship? I gave the crew plenty of time to get off before I shot the second torpedo."

"I don't know," one of the men replied. "Some left, but then the captain told them to come back aboard because the ship wasn't sinking."

"But he must have known a U-boat wouldn't leave him afloat unless there were escorts around. It was stupid to just sit there and wait to be killed!" Schulz told him, angry and upset by the unnecessary loss of life.

"Keep your eyes peeled for planes," Henke gruffly told the lookouts who were staring at the pitiful survivors on the raft. "If one comes along we'll be in worse shape than they are, because God knows we won't have time to dive."

Schulz sent for cigarettes, water, and cognac for the men on the raft. "I can't take you aboard," he told them. "It's against my orders. And too, we have a long patrol ahead of us."

"Herr Kaleu'nt!" a shout from one of the lookouts interrupted him. "Ship bearing one four o!"

Schulz dropped the line back onto the raft and said, "We've got to go now, but we'll come back and give you directions to land." Then he turned and shouted to the bridge, "Come to course one four o, full speed both diesels!"

The U-boat roared away, leaving the raft and its bewildered occupants, who never expected to see it again. The chase after the ship was futile, however, and a few hours later U-124 returned to the raft.

"I'm sorry I can't take you with us," Schulz again

told the survivors, "but you aren't far from land. The current will carry you in in about three days."

Brinker was standing beside the commander. "Herr Kaleu," he said in German, "we're a good 200 miles from the coast."

"I know it," Schulz replied. "But I can't tell them that. It seems so hopeless they wouldn't have the heart to even try."

"Do you think they have a chance?" Brinker asked quietly.

Schulz shook his head. "I don't know. Maybe." He paused. "But I doubt it."

He turned back to the men on the raft. "Good luck," he said in English. "I hope you make it."

The U-boat men watched silently until the raft became a tiny speck on the sea, and finally disappeared.

For the next two days, the commander was a different man, a stranger to his crew. Distant and preoccupied, he spoke little, and when he did, his tone and words were coldly cutting.

One of the younger boys, on his first cruise, came to Leo Raudzis confused and a little hurt. "Bootsmann," he said, "you know nobody can get around on a U-boat without bumping into other people. But just now when I accidentally brushed against the Old Man he nearly bit my head off."

"Forget it, kid," Raudzis told him. "It's those men on the raft. Sometimes you get sick of this business of killing. You'll find out."

"Well why couldn't we have brought them aboard?" the boy asked. "They wouldn't have taken up that much room. And you know they'll never make it to shore."

"Because it's against orders, that's why," Raudzis said flatly. "Sure you hate to leave them out there to die. We all do, the commander most of all." He shrugged. "But that's war, and you might as well get used to it."

Fritz Rafalski looked up. "Our commander knows his crew, and he knows we're with him a solid thousand per cent. He'll be all right. Just try to stay out of his way for awhile."

"Did you know Willem disobeyed orders by stopping to give them provisions?" asked Kesselheim, who had been listening to the conversation. "Uncle Karl told all the commanders they couldn't stop to help survivors if it put their boats in danger, and you know this place is crawling with planes!"

Rafalski laughed shortly. "Try explaining that to the Big Lion. 'Sorry, Herr Admiral, I lost my boat and killed my crew because I stopped to help three Britishers on a life raft,' 'I see. And what were they doing on the raft in the first place?' 'Because I blew their ship out from under them with two nicely placed torpedoes.' Crazy, isn't it?"

The boy shook his head. "It's all crazy to me."

Raudzis laughed and patted him on the shoulder. "Don't let it get you down. You'll get used to it. And if you're a good boy and the Wabos don't get you, it'll all be over a hundred years from now and you can go home and live happily ever after."

"Kesselheim," the commander called. "I can't find my other glove. Have you seen it?"

"I'm coming," Kesselheim replied. He hunted through the commander's locker, and in a few minutes came up with the missing glove in his hand.

"It had fallen in your boot," he said in reply to the puzzled look on Schulz's face.

He handed the glove to him. "Let me get you a cup of coffee, sir," he said.

Schulz started to shake his head.

"It's nice and fresh and hot," Kesselheim coaxed gently.

"All right," Schulz said. "I'll drink it in here."

A few minutes later Kesselheim returned with the coffee and a thick slice of cake. "Smutje sent you this," he said. "He just made it a little while ago. See? It's still warm."

The commander smiled. "Thanks, Kesselheim. And thank the cook for me, please."

By the next day Schulz had shaken off the depression that had engulfed him since the encounter with the men on the raft. He had done what he had to do, both in disregarding his orders when he stopped to help them, and later in leaving them to their fate in the Atlantic on an open raft. It was over now.

It was 1608 hours when the ship first came in sight. Schulz turned on a new course and began the long and exacting task of bringing his boat around for an attack.

After four hours he submerged and fired one torpedo. It missed.

The freighter, now warned, altered course and tried to escape by zig-zagging. She signaled on the 600-meter band that she was under attack by a submarine and gave her name, MARLENE.

Twilight had reduced visibility, so Schulz surfaced to race ahead for another shot. It took three more hours to get in position for a surfaced attack, and Schulz fired another single shot.

He waited while the seconds ticked by, marking the progress of the sleek torpedo.

"Hit!" the bridge watch shouted in chorus.

The torpedo exploded amidships, directly under the bridge. The ship seemed to stagger momentarily as the deep-throated roar of the detonation rumbled heavily across the water. But she did not sink.

Schulz waited with growing impatience. He had already spent seven hours chasing the MARLENE, and it was beginning to look as though she led a charmed life.

Wiping the sweat out of his eyes, he raised his binoculars to stare at the dark hulk now lying motionless.

"Fire three!" he ordered, fatigue giving a sharp edge to his voice.

The torpedo hit below the after mast, and the men on the U-boat's bridge waited. In spite of two gaping holes torn in her hull, the ship still miraculously floated.

"Herr Kaleu ..." Mohr said, not taking his eyes from his binoculars as he studied the water around the stopped ship.

Following his I.WO's gaze, Schulz saw the faint outline of something on the quiet sea. He stared, puzzled, at the vague shape.

"Wood," he murmured at last. "But of course!" Now he suddenly understood why the battered freighter would not sink.

"A cargo of wooden planks!" Mohr said. "So that's it."

The commander nodded grimly. "They won't sink, but by God, they'll burn."

He ordered the gun crew on deck and pumped twelve rounds of incendiaries into the stationary target.

The MARLENE caught fire and burned briefly. But almost at once the fires began to dwindle and soon were merely isolated flickers on the dark hull.

"Damn!" the commander muttered to himself, rubbing the back of his fist across his eyes. "Fire another fish, Mohr."

Mohr frowned into the sights. The forlorn ship with

the flames still winking an occasional red gleam across the water had put up a game fight to stay afloat.

The U-boat lurched as the fourth torpedo shot out of the tube. It hit the ship directly under her stack, and a great curtain of water rose over her.

The officers and men on the U-boat's bridge watched, silent and unmoving, as the MARLENE slowly settled by the stem and slid, almost without a ripple, into the calm sea. It was past midnight.

On April 8, U-124 met the TWEED, a 2,697 ton British freighter. Schulz circled around ahead for a submerged attack, and fired one torpedo.

"She's hit!" he called out from the periscope, and he watched to see if she would sink without another shot.

Without warning, the freighter wheeled abruptly and headed straight for the U-boat.

"My God!" yelped Schulz. "She's a Q-ship! Take her down! 2A plus 60! Full speed, hard port!"

As the freighter turned toward the U-boat, Schulz was sure he had stirred up a hornet's nest. The luckless U-boat that attacked one of these decoys usually found himself with more trouble than he could handle.

Disguised as merchantmen, the shabbier the better, and loaded with cork or balsa so that it was all but impossible to sink them, these anti-submarine ships carried fast engines, a navy crew, and all the detection gear and weapons that could be stuffed on board. Their general appearance tended to inspire overconfidence and carelessness in an attacker, but if the U-boat commander made a mistake, it was usually his last.

Schulz cursed the ship he had attacked and himself for a fool to blunder into it. Finally, when no counterattack came, he slowed down to listen. There was nothing to be heard. He ordered the boat to periscope depth for a cautious look around. The sea was empty. He looked again, and saw three small dots in the water where the ship had been. Lifeboats.

Feeling a little foolish after his headlong departure, he surfaced and returned to the nearest dot. The lifeboat was overturned and damaged, and of the men clinging precariously to it, several were injured.

Schulz brought his boat alongside, and his men helped the Britishers on board. The survivors stared numbly at the edelweiss on the conning tower as the Germans moved quickly and efficiently around them. Dr. Goder attended to the casualties while the U-boat crew righted and hastily repaired the lifeboat. The provisions for it had been lost, so Schulz gave them food, water, cognac, and cigarettes, and the exhausted survivors rested on the U-boat deck.

One of the Britishers had suffered a dislocated shoulder and a broken leg. He lay on the deck almost delirious from pain. Dr. Goder was kneeling beside him when the commander came over to him.

"Are you finished?" he asked.

"No, sir," Goder replied. "The muscles won't relax until the pain is relieved, and I can't put the shoulder back in place or set his leg until then."

"How long will that be?" Schulz demanded impatiently.

"Only a minute, sir. I've already given him a shot of morphine."

Dr. Goder waited for the drug to take effect, anxiously looking at his watch. Then he plunged a second syringe into the man's arm. Still the white-faced Britisher moaned in agony, his eyes glazed with pain.

Again Schulz clattered down the ladder. "Doctor," he implored frantically, "for God's sake hurry up!"

"Herr Kaleu, I'm doing all I can," Goder said. "I've

already given him enough morphine to knock a horse out. But you can see for yourself it's had no effect."

"We've got the lifeboat fixed, put provisions in it, and rigged the sails. We're just waiting for this man now," the commander told him.

"Herr Kaleu, he should have been unconscious a long time ago," Goder said helplessly.

Then he picked up a third syringe of morphine. "My friend," he said softly, "I'm going to knock you out if I have to do it with my fist."

The German words meant nothing to the suffering man, but the gentleness in the doctor's voice and touch was unmistakable.

The triple dose of morphine had the general effect of being hit over the head with a club, and the man was out cold before Goder pulled the needle out of his arm.

It was then only a matter of minutes until the shoulder was put back in place and the leg set and wrapped securely in splints. The man was lifted gently, still unconscious, into the lifeboat, while Dr. Goder gave instructions for his care to the other Britishers.

The commander gave a course to land to Mr. Baker, third officer of the TWEED, and the Britishers shoved off with grateful thanks to the men on the U-boat.

It had been an episode full of surprises to the British seamen. When told to come aboard the U-boat, some of them had expected to be killed. Others had expected to be taken prisoner. None had expected to be given cigarettes, cognac, and to be treated with sympathetic consideration. After his cold-blooded and brutally efficient torpedo attack, the U-boat commander had deliberately, and paradoxically, placed his boat in danger in order to save their lives.

They didn't know, as they pulled away from the

U-boat, if they would ever see England again, but they all knew that if they did, it would be because of a U-boat skipper to whom a shipwrecked sailor was no longer an enemy.

As Schulz watched the boat push off, he was sure he had seen the last of her occupants. But after the war, Third Officer (now Captain) Baker, unable to forget the U-boat commander whose compassion had saved his life, was determined to find him if he was still alive.

Knowing neither the number of the boat nor her commander's name, he could only base his inquiries on her edelweiss, which he mistook for a sun or a sunflower. With only this scrap of erroneous information to go on, he managed finally to track down Schulz's name and address in Hamburg, and wrote to him, asking if he were the same captain who had sunk the TWEED.

When Schulz replied that he was, Baker invited him and his wife to visit him in Poole. So sixteen years after the fateful encounter off the African coast, the two men clasped hands on the dock at Poole.

It was a strange and joyful reunion as the German couple was welcomed and feted by the Britishers. The act of mercy that had for a moment pushed the war aside to save the lives of shipwrecked sailors touched the hearts of the people of Poole, who had for hundreds of years known well the perils of the sea.

Schulz learned from Baker that the TWEED's sudden turn toward him that had alarmed him so was merely the result of loss of steering. His torpedo had knocked out her rudder, and the involuntary maneuver was far from an attack.

Schulz also learned the fate of the three men who had survived the sinking of the UMONA only to face a heartbreaking ordeal on a flimsy raft. The man who had a head injury had died a few days later, but the other two reached the African coast after 14 grueling days. Both of them, Edward Elliott and F. Brothers, wrote their thanks to Schulz after the war. Without provisions from the U-boat, they could not have survived.

Shortly before the TWEED sank, her radio operator had managed to get off an SOS. No acknowledgement or reply was picked up by the U-124.

Perhaps the plane had heard and responded to the distress signal, or maybe it was just a routine patrol. Wherever it came from, it spied the U-boat first and came out of the sun to attack.

"AIRCRAFT!"

Werner Henke, who had the bridge watch, decided it was already too late to dive, and it would be better to try to dodge the first rack of bombs.

He had underestimated the initiative of the L.I. two decks below him. When Brinker heard the lookout's frantic shout, he at once put the boat in a crash dive.

While Henke hesitated, the lookouts (knowing Brinker) fled down the hatch without waiting to be told. The last one grabbed the watch officer and shoved him hastily through the hatch while he dogged the cover shut.

Henke, confused and off balance, landed like a sack of potatoes on the control room deck. He grabbed the ladder as the boat put her nose down in a 20-degree diving angle.

"What's the trouble?" Mohr asked, laughing uproariously as Henke's feet slid out from under him. "You ought to be used to a Brinker Dive by now!"

"I'm going to break that damned L.I.'s neck," Henke muttered.

The bombs exploded above them with a force that

knocked all of them off their feet. The electric motors abruptly stopped, the lights went out, the depth gauge broke, and shattered glass whizzed through the control room like shrapnel. Everything not fastened down was violently thrown about as the boat took the full force of the explosions. The pressure from the concussion jammed one of the forward torpedoes so tightly in its tube that it could not be removed until the boat returned to base.

The bombs had landed exactly where the foreship would have been were it not for the steep down angle, and was as close a hit as she could have taken and survived.

With the motors off, the diving planes could not hold the boat, and Brinker trimmed her by ordering "everybody forward" and "everybody aft," shifting the weight of the men to keep her horizontal.

Obermaschinist Luft, who knew his electric motors better than a housewife knows her kitchen, set to work by the dim light of the emergency lamps. His skilled hands had coaxed them back to life by the time Brinker had trimmed the boat.

The lights flashed on again, revealing the wreckage in the control room. Broken glass and shreds of cork lay everywhere, and the air was thick with powder smoke although the hull was not damaged. It was a phenomenon Kesselheim noted with amazement, having heard about it from other crews but not believing it possible.

The list of kills grew steadily as the edelweiss boat relentlessly hunted and destroyed ships going in and out of the Freetown area. Enemy traffic was plentiful, and although air cover was a constant danger and a nuisance to the U-boat, she still sank the fast, single-traveling ships with torpedoes and her murderous deck gun until her supplies and munitions were nearly exhausted.

An occasional neutral ship, like the Spanish EL MONTECILLO, was stalked by the silent ruthless boat, then left to go on her way when identified. Other ships, not neutral, like the Dutch ATCINOUS, were lucky enough to dodge the first torpedo and could make good their escapes, meantime broadcasting their plight to other ships in the area. All enemy ships sailed on sharp zig-zag courses.

On April 13, U-124 turned her bow again toward Lorient. But thoughts of home and leave were soon swept away by the familiar cry of "Ship in sight!"

Soon after the chase began, the boat was forced under by an airplane.

"I think he saw us," Schulz, sitting at the periscope in the narrow conning tower, muttered disgustedly. "I'll take another look in a minute if we don't hear any bombs."

Willi Klein, packed in close beside him as helmsman, turned around and said, "Remember, Herr Kaleu, it was just a year ago today that one of those damn bees got us in the ass?"

"What?" asked Schulz in surprise. "Is today the 13th?"

"Yes, sir," answered Willi, "and it's the same time of day, too . . . 13 hours."

Schulz called down the hatch, "Take her down to 50 meters, L.I. We'll give this bee time to leave."

Ill-concealed grins were exchanged in the conning tower as the men wondered in amusement whether their commander's sudden decision was based on superstition or strategy. He did not elaborate.

A short while later, the boat took up the chase again. The freighter was still in sight, and the plane was gone. By dark, Schulz had narrowed the distance between himself and the freighter, and was racing full speed in order to get in a shot before the ship reached the British mine fields approaching Freetown.

"Herr Kaleu'nt," Rafalski called out from the radio shack. "She's spotted us! I just picked up a signal."

"What does she say?" Schulz called back.

"Says she's being followed by a submarine. She's the CORINTHIC."

Mohr quickly thumbed through the pages of ships listings. "Here she is, Herr Kaleu. British steamer CORINTHIC, 4,823 tons."

Through the dark night the two gradually came together; the freighter desperately signaling her plight and the silent U-boat, relentlessly closing in, torpedoes ready.

"Poor old fellows," remarked Kesselheim in sudden sympathy. "It must be hell up there, knowing a German U-boat is chasing them and just waiting for a fish to hit."

"Better them than us," someone replied callously.

"Yeah, sure."

Shortly before midnight, a torpedo sent her to the bottom and silenced her pathetic cries for help.

"Set our course for Lorient, Mohr," the commander said. "Let's go home."

Chapter Seven

On May 1, U-124 steamed into Lorient at the end of her longest and most successful war cruise. Twelve small flags, each bearing the tonnage of a merchantman she had sunk, floated gaily in the spring breeze alongside the commander's pennant. A crowd of people lined the quay, the band was playing, and girls stood, their arms loaded with flowers to present to the returning heroes. To one side stood the Big Lion, aloof and silent, but with unmistakable pride flashing in his ice-blue eyes.

German fortunes were running high, and the arrival of the victorious U-boat was a further cause for celebration. Greece had surrendered to Germany a week before, and Rommel, in a breath-taking drive, had outrun his supplies to halt at the Egyptian border. The slender grey boat at the pier seemed symbolic of the hard-fighting and victorious German forces everywhere.

Schulz stood with his officers on the U-boat's bridge, savoring the moment of triumph. Within minutes they would be tied up at the dock, and he could relax, relieved for awhile of the awesome responsibility of command of a ship in wartime. He could well smile with satisfaction. He had brought his boat and crew safely home after more than two months in enemy waters, 12 ships with some 57,626 tons under their belt. The fighting was over for awhile; it was time now for flowers and medals, honors, and a well-earned rest.

The admiral's aide came aboard as soon as the lines were made fast. As he and Schulz exchanged salutes, his horrified glance fell on the home-made Knight's Cross around the commander's neck, and he said with undisguised disapproval, "Get that thing off immediately! The admiral's coming on board to give you the real one!"

Schulz silently removed the medal, and if he perhaps considered the one from his crew the "real" one, he at least refrained from saying so.

U-124's crew stood at proud attention through the brief ceremony as "Uncle Karl" presented their commander with the Knight's Cross to the Iron Cross, and cheered him when Schulz dismissed them, his eyes shining, the black and silver cross gleaming at his throat.

So now the old man was officially an ace, the crew noted with satisfaction. As far as they were concerned, he had been an ace for a long time, and they were pleased by the official recognition. He was a good commander, concerned with the welfare of his crew, performing his own job always competently, often brilliantly.

They had sometimes heard other crews say contemptuously of their own skippers that "he has a sore throat," an infrequent but not unknown malady among U-boat commanders that could only be relieved by prompt application of the black and white ribbon of the Knight's Cross around the neck.

For Schulz there remained only one hurdle, and it was at hand as he stepped aside for the admiral to precede him into the little wardroom. It was time now to tell the admiral that he, a trusted U-boat commander wearing a shiny new medal, had deliberately disobeyed orders and placed his boat in considerable jeopardy to rescue British survivors. He did not know how Dönitz would react, and he made no effort to justify himself, but simply and briefly told him what had happened.

The admiral's penetrating blue eyes probed deeply into his own while he asked question after question about the encounters. "Had the ships gotten off signals giving their positions?" "Yes." "Had he noticed many patrol planes in the area?" "Yes." "How long did he have his boat stopped?" "Too long."

Dönitz sat quiet and thoughtful for a moment. The risk had been too great. Nevertheless, Schulz had acted correctly. The admiral approved.

The tension suddenly drained out of the commander and he smiled with relief. Disobedience did not come lightly to a man of his background and training. He poured cognac for the admiral and himself and they drank to the successful cruise just completed.

Next day a parade was held to present other decorations, and Rolf Brinker was awarded the Gold Cross, the first man in the flotilla and one of the first three or four in the entire navy to receive this high-ranking medal.

The commander went home on leave, and the rest of the crew was soon scattered over Germany for six weeks while the boat underwent a much-needed overhauling.

Brinker and Goder left together that night on the train to Kiel, the first stop on their way to Berlin where the entire crew of U-124 were to be guests of the city and attend the premiere of a movie about U-boats. After that, they planned to go to Mohr's wedding.

The three young officers, all the same age, were close friends. As shipmates on U-124, they had come to know each other intimately, and watch-free hours were filled with outspoken conversation ranging from the overall stupidity of war to the most satisfactory ways of spending a leave in Berlin. There were few subjects that failed to intrigue their keen and inquisitive minds, and none that escaped the sharp edge of Mohr's wit. Bold and self-assured, they talked and laughed, their discussions spiked with wit and strongly underlined by Mohr's penetrating sense of the ridiculous.

The bond of affection, especially between Mohr and Brinker, was grounded in a shrewd and accurate appraisal of each other's temperament and ability. This mutual confidence and rapport would serve U-124 well in months to come.

Goder had recently married, so he was pleased to give Mohr multifarious advice, helpful and otherwise, and he and Brinker were to be with their comrade as he took this momentous step into matrimony.

When the train left Lorient, the air was warm and sticky, and Goder had opened the window in his sleeping compartment. As they sped north during the night, the weather changed abruptly, and long before they reached Kiel, a cold rain had set in. Goder, in an exhausted sleep under the open window, had taken a severe cold by morning. Furious, but too ill to make the trip to Berlin, he remained in Keil while the others went on without him.

The U-124's crew was loudly cheered by the enthusiastic crowd at the theater, but the overdone and melodramatic heroics of their counterparts on the screen left them all feeling somewhat silly, and they were glad when it was over.

This had been Werner Henke's last cruise on board the U-124, and he said goodbye to his shipmates. This handsome blue-eyed blond departed on his leave full of anticipation and happy plans that would further enhance his well-earned reputation of devastating success with the ladies.

Henke,[1] like Schulz, Gunther Prien, and several other well-known U-boat commanders, had come to the navy from merchant ships, having been a sailor since he was 15. Like them, he would prove himself a consummate seaman and a bold and skillful commander. And as the veteran ace skipper of U-515, he would wear the Knight's Cross with Oak Leaves.

Dutifully accompanied by Brinker, the beaming Mohr was married to his Eva, a beautiful girl with

---

1. On the night of April 8–9, 1944, Henke was surprised on the surface near Madeira by U.S. Naval aircraft from the escort carrier USS GUADALCANAL. He crash-dived to escape the bombs, but the planes from this hunter-killer group were already alerting Captain Dan Gallery on the GUADALCANAL, and within minutes he had the destroyer escorts FLAHERTY and PILLSBURY speeding to the position. PILLSBURY soon had a sonar contact, and made two hedgehog attacks. The other two DE's in the group, CHATELAIN and POPE, arrived a few minutes later, effectively boxing in the U-515, which was soon forced to surface under the plastering from the four destroyers.

Henke, however, was not through fighting, and his own deck gunners opened fire about the same time as the destroyers. It was a fierce battle, with shells flying thick and fast, but the U-515 was hopelessly outclassed, and sank only a few minutes later, following an internal explosion. Thirty-seven of the crew and all six officers, including the commander, were picked up by the destroyers.

Henke was later shot and killed in a suicidal attempt to escape from a POW camp near Washington, D.C. Even today, there is bitter and perplexed speculation by those who knew him as to the reason for his foolhardy flight which he must have known would almost inevitably result in his death.

pale golden hair and fascinating green eyes. He had proposed to her on his previous leave in the preposterously inappropriate setting of a sidewalk cafe along the Kufurstendamm in Berlin at high noon, shouting to be heard above the traffic noises around them.

After a short honeymoon, they spent two months at Neustadt, a village on the Baltic Sea, where Mohr attended the commanders' school. The next cruise was to be Schulz's last, and he had recommended Mohr to replace him as commander. It was an idyllic time for the young couple, who in the two years of their marriage would be together for only about seven months.

The crew came back to Lorient during the first week in July, and left on patrol on the 10th.

Heinz Eck replaced Mohr as I.WO, making only this one cruise on U-124. The II.WO was Hans Köster, a bright young officer with the unlikely nickname of "Umo" (Unser Mop, an affectionate name for a shaggy dog). Brinker as L.I. and an engineer pupil rounded out the complement of officers.

The boat left Lorient on July 10, but had to return to base the next day on account of engine trouble. Repairs took several more days, and she left again on the 15th, heading south as soon as she cleared the Bay of Biscay.

As she cruised along parallel to the Spanish coast, a lookout spotted an object in the water ahead of them. They approached it cautiously, and could soon make out that it was a buoy.

"It must have broken loose from its moorings," Schulz remarked to Köster. "And it could cause a lot of damage if a boat happened to hit it."

He leaned over the conning tower hatch. "Gun crew to the upper deck!" he called.

The target practice was a welcome bit of variety,

but was over almost before it began, for the sharp-eyed gunners dispatched the buoy in a matter of seconds.

The commander, in a jovial mood, hastily scribbled a signal to be gotten off at once to the BdU: *"Versenkt eine Tonne."*

The German word for buoy is *Tonne* and so is the word for ton.

U-124 was put in a wolf pack along with U-109, U-123, U-93, and U-94, and the five boats cruised in a patrol line southward toward the Moroccan coast. They searched without any success, until on August 10, they received a signal from U-97 directing them to a convoy (HG 69) near Gibraltar.

On August 11, U-79 and the Italian boats FINZI and MARCONI, which were also in the vicinity, joined the hunt, U-79 making contact with the convoy that same day. U-124 headed for the reported position, both diesels on full speed.

Just before noon, an approaching plane sent her under in a crash dive. When she surfaced half an hour later, U-331 was in sight. The two boats pulled alongside each other so the commanders could exchange news.

U-331 was under the command of von Tiesenhausen, who three months later would sink the British battleship BARHAM. He told Schulz that he had received a signal from a Condor giving him a bearing on the convoy, but that he had not found it. About an hour later, U-109 came close by, but her commander, Bleichrodt, was able to offer no further information, and the boats continued their search.

Soon afterward, Schulz received a position report from U-94 as the latter was going in to attack. He set his course to intercept, and reached the convoy's estimated position after dark about three hours later. The only sign of the convoy, however, was a destroyer which headed toward the boat, then turned away to the north.

Schulz and the other boats searched stubbornly for the convoy, painstakingly evaluating, plotting, and following every clue.

The crews, in a constant state of battle-readiness, ate and slept when they could. Convoy battles frequently lasted for days on end, and U-boat men quickly learned to take advantage of every possible minute of sleep, being unconscious as soon as they were horizontal.

Schulz set his course according to the latest information, and for the first time in nearly 24 hours, stretched out on his bunk.

He had been asleep for two and a half hours when Kesselheim shook him gently.

"Herr Kommandant . . ."

A picture of the somewhat more abrupt awakenings in the crew's tiered bunks in the forward torpedo room suddenly crossed Kesselheim's mind—a slap across the backside and a loud shout, "All right, all right, do you want to sleep your life away? Get up and earn your pay, you lazy lout!" and he wondered how Willem would react to a similar greeting.

Schulz sat up, rubbing his eyes, as Kesselheim, finding the notion wildly funny, grinned at him.

"Signal from U-331, Herr Kaleu," he said, trying to stifle the idiotic impulse to laugh as he handed the paper to Schulz.

Schulz, still groggy, wondered what Kesselheim found so hilarious at 1:30 in the morning, but forgot about it as he scanned the message from von Tiesenhausen. U-331 had reached the convoy, but was driven under by three destroyers. He gave his position.

Schulz pulled on his boots, and Kesselheim handed

him a steaming mug of coffee. Knowing the commander's sleep would be over as soon as he read the signal, Kesselheim had brought the coffee with him.

Von Tiesenhausen's position report indicated that the convoy was close, and Schulz altered course to search the area in wide sweeps. Reports from other boats and an occasional Condor gave direction to the search, but the convoy, frustratingly close, remained out of reach of the pack.

Successive position reports necessitated careful plots and clear judgment to evaluate them, and left the commander no time for even a brief nap. Fatigue dragged at him until his hard narrow bunk a few feet away seemed as grand and remote as a palace.

Long hours of hunting stretched into days, and days and nights ran together in a continuous jumble of intercepted reports, calculations, plots, and guesses —and only the convoy mattered.

On the bridge, Schulz searched the empty horizon in the gathering dusk and puzzled over the convoy's position.

"Aircraft! Bearing one two five!" Hennig shouted behind him.

Schulz found the approaching plane and studied it for a second. The wings were high; it was no Condor.

"Alarm!" he yelled. "Dive! Dive!"

There was no time to wait and see if it had spotted the U-boat. The men on the bridge jumped through the hatch as the boat started down.

A scream of pain from the engine room carried above the ordered confusion of the crash dive and brought Dr. Goder running through the maze of men and machines, struggling against the steep down angle. By the time the boat had leveled off, he had reached the injured Maschinistmaat Struwe.

The little finger of his left hand was badly crushed,

and Goder needed only the briefest examination before telling the commander that he would have to
operate immediately. Narcotics eased the blinding
pain, and Goder worked on Struwe's mangled hand
while the boat remained submerged and still. The
boat lost her speed underwater, but she rode too
roughly on the surface for Goder to have even at-
tempted to repair the man's hand, so Schulz kept her
submerged until he had finished.

By 2030 hours, the injured machinist was asleep in
his bunk, his hand bandaged and the pain dulled by
morphine, and U-124 was back on the surface. A
signal from Reinhard Hardegen in U-123 reported
contact with the convoy and gave a fix. It was close.

Schulz balanced himself against the rolling motion
of the boat as she plowed into the swells. He frowned,
fighting back the exhaustion that turned his legs to
lead and made every thought and movement an
effort. Since they had started after the convoy days
ago, his only sleep and rest had been in brief snatches
constantly broken by new reports on circumstances
that required his decisions.

"Clear the bridge!" he ordered.

If nothing could be seen, perhaps something might
be heard. The sound of the convoy's screws might
carry through the water to give a fix.

Schroeder sat at the sound gear, slowly turning it
around the compass while he strained to catch the
faintest sound through the earphones. Finally he
looked up at the commander who stood watching him
intently, trying to read his face for some sign of the
merchantmen.

"Nothing, Herr Kaleu," Schroeder said. "Not a
sound."

"Very well." Schulz turned and motioned to Brinker. "Bring her up."

He waited, his hand on the steel ladder as the boat came back to the surface and Brinker said, "Conning tower clear, sir."

Schulz opened the hatch and jumped onto the dripping bridge, quickly scanning the sky and horizon before calling the bridge watch up. The moment a U-boat surfaced was always a dangerous one as she came up blind. So the diving tanks were not blown and the boat remained heavy and ready for an emergency crash dive. The commander, alone on the bridge, took a first quick look for danger while the lookouts waited below him in the conning tower.

A dark shape to the south caught his eye, and he watched as the destroyer wheeled in close, but not directly toward the boat. Schulz waited, his hand on the hatch cover, as a second destroyer swept along close behind.

'Hunting group,' he thought, watching the ships as they careened along, wildly zig-zagging. 'As long as they don't come much closer . . .'

The destroyers zagged away, and he yelled down the hatch, "Bridge watch up!"

Only seconds after the lookouts were in position, Klein caught sight of two small shapes on the water— U-boats.

"Come to course 300 degrees," Schulz ordered.

The boat had followed her new heading for scarcely a half hour when a lookout shouted, "Convoy!"

Day was already breaking as the boat roared toward the convoy, both diesels on full speed. There was still time to attack.

"U-boat zero degrees!" reported a lookout.

While Schulz watched the boat ahead of them, a shout of "Aircraft at 180 degrees!" spun him around.

"Sunderland!" he yelled. "Dive! Dive!"

The U-boat was already starting to submerge as the

lookouts scrambled through the hatch, Schulz on their heads. He held onto the ladder under the hatch, waiting to see if the plane would drop bombs. There were none. Perhaps she had not seen them.

The U-124 came back to the surface and resumed her course of 300 degrees. In rapid succession she met the Italian boat FINZI, another German boat that was surfacing, and the Italian MARCONI.

A few minutes later a Condor flew over and gave the boats a new bearing for the convoy. After steering 340 degrees and 315 degrees for some two hours, a lookout spotted the mast of a destroyer, followed by smoke. The convoy.

Schulz closed in on the merchantmen, avoiding the destroyers that zig-zagged around them. For the first time since the hunt had started for this elusive convoy, he was close to an attacking position. But again a destroyer came toward the boat, and he was forced to give way. Before he could get back to the convoy, another destroyer had come up with a searchlight. Baffled and exhausted after five days virtually without sleep, Schulz again lost the convoy.

On the morning of August 15, the wolf pack, still doggedly hunting, was still without success. Although the convoy, moving like a will-o-the-wisp, gave only occasional and insubstantial glimpses to its enemies, these waters some 300 sea miles west of Finisterre, were well populated. U-boats met each other, Italian boats, British destroyers, the Luftwaffe Condors, and RAF Sunderlands with almost boring frequency. U-93, U-79, U-331, U-371, U-94, U-123, U-126, the Italians FINZI and MARCONI, and U-124 all had been repeatedly chased and forced under or off course by destroyers. Signaling sighting reports to each other to keep the convoy under surveillance, the wolf pack hunted like the well-trained team they were and

stuck to the merchantmen with obstinate persever-
ance. But they still found it impossible to attack.

Finally the wolves were called off and the convoy
operation broken off as a total failure on the 16th.
The radar-equipped escorts had kept a whole pack of
experienced and battle-wise U-boats at bay for a
week without losing a single ship from the convoy.
Although the drained and disgusted U-boat commanders did not know it, it was a preview of the
difficulties and dangers that would beset the U-boat
force when practically all escorts would be so
equipped.

After the wolf pack was dispersed, U-124 made a
short foray around the Azores and Cape Finisterre.
Here again her luck was nil, as she managed to get a
shot at only one freighter and missed that. Then she
was ordered back to Lorient, where Dönitz would
speak sympathetically of the bad luck on the operation, but would still give Schulz a rap on the knuckles for not reporting his own contacts with the convoy
sooner and more frequently.

They came through the Bay of Biscay in the usual
manner, submerged by day, surfacing only at night to
recharge the batteries. Brinker had instructed the
engineering pupil to hold the boat on 30 meters, and
he and Schulz sat in the wardroom playing chess.

Suddenly the chessmen fell over as the boat rolled,
and for a split second the commander and L.I. stared
at each other. A U-boat at 30 meters does not roll.

Brinker jumped to his feet in a headlong dash to
the control room where the manometer duly registered a deep wet 30 meters. He spun around and
jerked up the periscope. All around them was the
bright sunny Bay of Biscay.

"My God!" he squawked, "we're on the surface!"

Schulz had run into the control room right on

Brinker's heels, and now he shoved him roughly aside while he scanned the sea and sky around them. Nothing was in sight, and Schulz wondered painfully how long they had been cruising along on the surface, blind and exposed, without a soul on the bridge.

"Now if you please, Herr Brinker," he said, turning around, "TAKE HER DOWN!"

The trouble with the manometer was quickly cleared up. Someone had mistakenly closed the valve, so that no matter the depth or pressure, the gauge would register 30 meters.

Schulz and Brinker returned to the wardroom, but both of them had lost all interest in chess. Preoccupied with the picture of their boat running blind on the surface in these most heavily patrolled waters, they both wondered how many boats and their crews had gone to the bottom through just such a trivial mistake. It was a depressing line of thought, especially for a pair of tired, discouraged officers returning from an unsuccessful cruise.

For Schulz, it was the last war cruise, for he was being transferred to La Baule as commander of the 6th U-Flotilla.

Saying goodbye to his boat and crew in Lorient was an unexpectedly poignant moment for the commander. Many of the men had been with him since the ill-fated cruise of the U-64, and several more had come aboard on the U-124's first cruise. They had been through so much together, and he realized for the first time at this moment of parting how close he was to his crew.

They presented him with gifts, mementos they had carefully made from scraps of wood and metal and polished until they glowed, and tiny pennants, each marked with the name and tonnage of a ship he had sunk. He looked at their faces, so familiar to him, and found that he had to choke back the tears as he whispered his thanks. When he left the boat for the last time in Lorient, he took with him these small treasures along with his pennant.

As he gave his patrol report at headquarters, he was suddenly interrupted by the question, "Now what was this you sank? You never mentioned it again, and we cannot figure out what it could possibly have been."

"Sank?" Schulz asked, puzzled. "I didn't sink *anything.*"

"Then what about that signal?"

Schulz shook his head in confusion. "What signal?"

"This one!" And the scrap of paper was waved under his nose. "Sunk one ton!"

Schulz looked at it and burst out laughing. "That's one buoy," he explained, delighted by the uproar his signal had caused at headquarters as the perplexed staff officers tried to imagine what sort of one-ton vessels their U-boats were sinking.

Chapter Eight

Mohr had said goodbye to his weeping bride, and returned to Lorient to take command of the boat he knew and loved so well. Recently promoted, he now held the rank of Kapitänleutnant (full lieutenant), the youngest one in the navy at 24. His youth, however, and the fact that the officers who were now under his command had known him familiarly and well as a fellow junior officer was to prove no obstacle. These officers and the crew, many of whom were years older than their new commander, accepted his leadership confidently and wholeheartedly.

Mohr had a quick and brilliant mind, and his natural impulsive and rash tendency to plunge headlong into any situation, no matter how dangerous, was tempered somewhat by sound training and an instinctive grasp of U-boat tactics. His flair for leadership was phenomenal, and his crew was totally under the spell of this smart and sunny commander who seemingly could do no wrong and on whom the Fates seemed to lavish every gift.

Mohr, for his part, received the legacy of a sound and sturdy boat, hardened by battle in the bloody

Atlantic sea lanes, and a crew superbly trained and
molded together into a sharp and beautifully disciplined unit by Wilhelm Schulz.

The crew, as tough and battle-seasoned as the boat
herself, was a reliable group of individuals who had
learned not only to stand firm and steady in an emergency, but also in which emergencies they must act
instantly without orders, or even in defiance of orders. Mohr was sure there was not a better crew in
the entire U-boat service.

On September 16, U-124 left Lorient along with
U-201, commanded by Addi Schnee. Soon after clear-
ing the Bay of Biscay, both boats were directed onto
Convoy OG 74, from Gibraltar to Great Britain.

Early on the morning of September 20, the eager
shout came down from the lookouts on watch: "Commander to the bridge!"

Mohr silently observed the tell-tale wisp of smoke
astern, his eyes pressed to heavy binoculars. In a few
minutes he could tell that the ships, still invisible
except for the smoke, were heading eastwards. He
signaled his sighting report to the BdU, and was ordered to attack and keep reporting.

Toward midday, visibility began to diminish as a
light haze hung over the sun. Through the long afternoon, U-124 stuck doggedly to the small convoy, at
times losing contact, then regaining it, as the fast
escorts swung out in long sweeps around their
charges.

As twilight added a purplish cast to the deceptive
haze that had already ruined visibility, Mohr moved
still closer to the convoy. It was difficult to maintain
contact without being seen at this most critical time
of day, and the escorts, knowing this, and also knowing that a lurking U-boat would attack with the
darkness, increased their unpredictable sweeps

around the convoy to drive away any waiting boats. Once contact was lost in the gathering dusk, it might be lost for good.

At last it was dark enough to attack, and Mohr, seizing his first chance, slipped his boat into the convoy on the surface, about 600 meters behind the corvette that guarded the starboard side. Within minutes, three torpedoes were launched. Watching anxiously on the U-boat's bridge, the lookouts observed all three hits, and were able to see two of the ships sink. By this time, the escorts had lit up the battlefield with star shells, but U-124 remained undetected while Mohr brought her outside the convoy on the western side.

From the east came the distant rumbling of exploding depth charges. Was Schnee's boat catching it? U-124 steamed along in the darkness, easily holding contact with the starboard escort silhouetted against the light. As soon as things quieted down in the convoy, they would attack again.

Suddenly the escort turned, heading toward the U-boat, and Mohr fell back. The star shells went out, and the convoy altered course in the sudden darkness. Contact was lost.

Peter Zschech called to Mohr across the bridge. "Herr Kaleu, signal flare at 190 degrees!"

With a couple of steps Mohr was beside the I.WO. He studied the distant lights silently for a moment. "Decoys," he said finally. "They're trying to lure us away from the convoy."

He took one last sweep around the black horizon with his binoculars and ordered, "Clear the bridge! Make ready to dive!"

Submerged, they listened for the sounds of screws to betray the convoy which had long since slipped out of sight. But there was only silence around them, and the boat surfaced to take up the hunt again.

Throughout the rest of the night and the following day, U-124 searched in vain, occasionally diving to listen for the sound of screws. Nothing. Mohr called up headquarters to ask for air reconnaissance, and the radio man intercepted a message from Schnee reporting contact with the convoy, which was now steering southwards.

"Shadow on the port bow!"

"At last," muttered Mohr, studying the dim shapes gradually coming into sight.

As the boat closed, he could make out three freighters and one protecting corvette. Dodging the corvette, he wheeled his boat into position to attack.

"Couldn't be better, Zschech," he said breezily. "We'll fire at all three at once."

Zschech set up firing plots for the freighters as the distance narrowed between them. The first shadow moved into the crosshair and Zschech waited until it intersected her bridge.

"Torpedo . . ."

Before he could say the "los!" that would send six fish on their way, he was interrupted by the dull roar of three torpedo detonations rumbling across the black water. He looked at Mohr in confusion.

"Schnee!" Mohr growled through his teeth.

It was infuriating that the two boats had chosen the same targets at the same time and even more infuriating that it was Schnee's boat that claimed the prize.

Within minutes the freighters had disappeared, and the radio room intercepted a signal from Schnee to the BdU reporting his sinking of the three ships.

Dönitz then signaled the two prowling boats, telling Mohr to close in.

Mohr signaled back to say that he was already in

contact with the convoy, adding wryly that "*Schnee schoss schneller*." (Schnee shot faster.)

Three hours later, a message came from Dönitz to Mohr and Schnee telling them to head southward toward a new convoy reported by an Italian submarine, and to be on the lookout for these boats.

Late in the evening, another signal came from Dönitz: "To Mohr, Schnee: Gibraltar convoy mopped up. Cruise northward."

The Italian submarine TORELLI sighted a large convoy, the outgoing HG 73, west of Gibraltar. U-371, on her way into the Mediterranean, also reported seeing it, and held contact briefly. Then she continued on her way southward, and left the Italian boat shadowing.

TORELLI lost contact, but regained it on the 21st. Soon afterwards, she was spotted by the destroyer VIMY and forced under to be severely damaged by the destroyer's depth charges. On September 22, the BdU ordered U-Mohr and U-Schnee into the hunt.

On September 23, the Italian boat DA VINCI found the convoy, shadowing and sending back accurate position reports until the merchant ships changed course during the night. Using DA VINCI's reports, German air reconnaissance found the convoy the following morning in the vicinity of Cape Finisterre.

The aircraft observed that two ships were sinking and another one burning. They had apparently fallen victim to the Italian boat MALASPINA, since she was the only boat known to be in the immediate vicinity. The MALASPINA then must have been destroyed by the convoy's escorts, for she was missing since that time.

Meantime, U-124 and U-201 were closing in, setting

their courses from the various reports on the convoy's position that had been filling the air.

On the morning of September 25, Schnee gained contact and gave his position. Following his reports, Mohr came in sight of the convoy that same day near the entrance to St. George's Channel.

Weather conditions had worsened considerably, bringing little rain squalls which were convenient for dodging into when escorts came out, but which also served to conceal the convoy at times. It was necessary to exercise the utmost care since such rapidly shifting visibility conditions could cause them to run headlong into an escort before seeing her. A heavy following sea had forced the lookouts on the bridge to buckle themselves securely with their safety belts.

Lacking the speed to keep up with the huge swells, or the size and weight to cut through them, the U-boat labored doggedly as the seas shook her and shoved her along, now in a trough, now on the crest of a wave, trembling with a violent and different vibration as her screws came momentarily out of the water.

Occasionally a big wave would overtake the boat, sweeping relentlessly up over the after ship to completely cover the bridge and the men on watch. They could feel the gigantic force of the sea as it tore at their bodies, and they held their breath as the wave rolled over their heads. They would wonder frantically if their heavy leather safety belts would hold them safe against the terrifying strength of Rasmus, the sea god as he fought to claim them for his own.

Then it would be past, and they would emerge, spluttering and choking, and gasping with relief at being again above the water.

Mohr, caught up in the tingling excitement of the chase, laughed at them and at himself, all soaking wet. The primitive thrill of the hunt, intensified by the danger they all knew was waiting for them, swept through the whole boat, sharpening their senses to a peak of quick alertness. Visibility was no more than one mile.

The boat now sped through the convoy as Mohr brought her into attacking position. The bridge watch searched the seas around them, nerves straining. At this speed, inside a convoy, the danger of collision was far from merely theoretical, and each man knew his life might depend on how well he used his eyes.

"Destroyer on the port bow," Bootsmann Henning reported.

"Hard starboard!" Mohr called, turning away and back out of the convoy. By the time they had shaken off the destroyer, which had turned to follow, the convoy was lost again.

Turning back, Mohr tried to re-establish contact.

"Ship bearing 265 degrees," a lookout reported.

"Cruiser!" Mohr said, watching as the big ship wheeled and sped out of sight.

Mohr dived to pick up the sounds of the convoy, and was able to identify the cruiser's position on the boat's port bow, while the main body of the convoy was slightly abaft the port beam.

Back on the surface, Mohr again sighted the cruiser, some 2,000 meters ahead of the leading destroyer escort. He got off a spread of two torpedoes at the cruiser; both missed the sharply zig-zagging ship.

By now he was able to bring his boat into the convoy on a reciprocal course.

"Tanker, Zschech," Mohr pointed. The big tanker was well guarded by a destroyer and two smaller escorts close by. The destroyer, a little ahead of the tanker, was approaching fast.

"Try one fish for the destroyer," Mohr told the I.WO.

"Angle on the bow, 90 degrees," Zschech called out. "Distance 300 meters ..." The destroyer was at the minimum distance for a torpedo shot.

"Los!"

The destroyer altered her course, and the torpedo missed.

Zschech was already calling out figures for the attack on the tanker: "Angle 90 degrees ... distance 400 meters ... Tubes one and two ... Fire!"

The two torpedoes hit almost simultaneously—one forward, the other midships. The tanker sank by the bow.

A few minutes later, the U-Boat was out of the column of merchantmen, which vanished from sight in the rain.

Mohr signaled the BdU that he had just sunk a 12000-ton tanker, and minutes later received a reply from Dönitz containing one word: "Bravo!"

By the next night, the boat had regained contact, and soon after dark had slipped past the escorts.

"Destroyer, Herr Kaleu!" a lookout yelled. "On the port bow—*close!*"

Mohr turned, binoculars pressed to his eyes. The long sleek shape racing through the night was precisely on a collision course, and she was close. Close enough for them to see the white bone in her teeth that showed she was moving fast.

"Clear the bridge!" Mohr shouted. "Hard port!"

The bridge watch tumbled into the control room as though a trap door had been sprung under them.

"Destroyer! Collision course—she's almost on top of us!" they told Brinker.

"Come on, you idiot," Brinker whispered under his

breath, looking up and waiting for Mohr to appear in the hatch above him.

No one knew better than Brinker the value of even a split second in an emergency dive. The longer he waited to pull the plug, the closer it put them to that destroyer. A U-boat's safety, and their life or death, could be measured in meters at such a moment.

"Hard port," the helmsman's disciplined voice repeated, as unexcited as though they were pulling into their berth at Lorient.

Mohr now stood alone on the bridge, hands gripping the hatch cover, watching the destroyer as though bewitched. She had not changed her course. That meant she had not seen him. Yet.

Mohr had made his decision to stay on the surface and run the risk of being sighted. And by turning toward the destroyer instead of away, he had chosen the more dangerous course. They would pass each other at appallingly close range, but being on a reciprocal course, they would be past each other much more quickly. Mohr was gambling his life that the Britishers would not see him for that short time.

Now it was too late to dive. And if the destroyer should spot him now, she would ram him before he could turn away.

Mohr could see the white foam arching back from both sides of the knife-sharp prow as the destroyer lay bows-on to the U-boat. She looked enormous to him as she bore down as fast as a frieght train. And she was close. Too close!

"Dear God," he prayed frantically, "don't let them see us! Just this moment please, please!"

He felt he could reach out and touch the destroyer as she swept past on the starboard side, no more than 30 meters from him. He could make out every detail on her upper decks and bridge, the men looking in every direction but down. The moment was eternity!

Then she was past. The spell was broken, and Mohr called the bridge watch back up. They stared astonished at the destroyer still straight on her course, and the two wakes, side by side, so close together.

Mohr caught sight of Brinker's upturned face in the control room below him.

"They can't see us!" he yelled exultantly. "They're all blind!"

But Brinker knew the risk Mohr had taken, and regardless of the commander's jubilant boast, Brinker was horrified.

He shook his head. "God in Heaven," he muttered, half as an oath, half as a prayer.

The desperate risk Mohr had taken to stay on the surface paid off. By daylight of the next day, he had sent three ships to the bottom.

Shortly before dawn they sighted the U-203. Mützelburg had followed their position reports to the convoy. With daylight, the boats pulled out to shadow the convoy and hold contact until darkness fell again. The task was difficult and nervewracking. Storms and high seas hampered visibility and left the boat in plain view one minute, only to have every trace of the convoy disappear in the next.

Mohr flopped down on his bunk. Dog-tired, he was asleep by the time his eyes closed. He knew he would need all the rest he could get, for the battle was not over. When dark came again, he would attack, and he would need to be as alert and fresh as possible.

Unfortunately, he would manage to get only a few hours rest, and that was in short snatches. The problems of holding contact with the convoy would frequently require the commander's decision, and he would be waked up either by a hand on his shoulder and an apologetic voice, "Herr Kaleu?", or by the summary shout of "Commander to the bridge!" Either way, there would be no more sleep for awhile.

The day proved to be as demanding as the previous night had been, and twice as exhausting. In spite of all their efforts, they repeatedly lost the convoy. Then they would dive to listen for the sound of screws, or if these were too far away to be heard, Mohr would calculate the possible evasions the convoy might have made, circle them, and set his course on a tangent to this circle.

Wireless signals during the day indicated that U-Reschke had also made contact. Now there were four boats against the embattled convoy. The wolf pack closed in as daylight faded, 24 long gleaming torpedoes ready in their tubes, waiting only their final settings and the shout of "Torpedo, los!" to send them on their deadly mission.

The dark rough night with its cutting wind that sent spray flying over the open bridges and the brief angry rain squalls pelting down on them was suddenly turned into a holocaust as the first torpedo found its victim.

Mohr had just brought his boat past the port escort and found a target directly ahead of him. Peter Zschech was calling out the torpedo settings when another U-boat scored a hit.

The escorts wheeled toward the stricken ship, firing star shells which lit up the stormy sky with a strange and unholy brilliance. Mohr quickly looked around him.

"Nobody's seen us yet," he decided. "Fire a spread, Zschech, and hurry up!"

Their target was still on her course as the three torpedoes left the tubes in quick succession. As they watched, she turned slightly to port and increased her speed. But it was not enough to escape the whole spread, and one torpedo ripped into her stern section. She lost way and they could see her settling in the water as the U-boat turned.

Mohr glanced at the men around him on the bridge, floodlit by the glittering fireworks above them. He swung the boat around to head for the darkness outside the convoy, but, ever the opportunist, managed to get off a shot at one more freighter with his stern tubes as a parting gesture.

"Damn those flares," he muttered, reluctantly turning away from the merchant ships and their treacherous canopy of light. They would steam along parallel to them now and wait for the dark.

"Shadow off the starboard quarter!"

Mohr picked the destroyer out of the shadows. She was not coming directly for them, but she was close, and he had to give way.

"Port easy," he said. "Both diesels ahead slow."

Mohr fidgeted and waited, frustrated by the destroyer that had unwittingly forced him onto a reciprocal course to the convoy.

"Shadow off the port bow!"

Mohr turned around. There she was. Another damned escort. Did the British have a million of them, he wondered furiously. There was nothing for it, however, except to turn away, and this he did, cursing earnestly and fluently.

The star shells had gone out now, but U-124 was a long way from an attacking position. Mohr set her course to circle back to the front of the convoy, and the boat shuddered through the waves at full speed.

Mohr dropped through the hatch and clattered down the ladder into the control room with a shout of, "Hey, L.I.!"

"Here I am," Brinker answered, at his elbow.

"Listen, Brinker," Mohr told him, "I've got to have more speed."

"They're running full speed now," Brinker replied, "but I'll see what I can do. Maybe another knot or two."

Mohr looked pensive. "Wait a minute, Rolf," he said.

As frequently happened with these two old friends, they now chose to ignore the gulf between commander and subordinate, and talked on an equal footing.

"What's the fastest she'll go?" Mohr asked.

Knowing Mohr, Brinker was instantly on his guard, wondering what was going on behind the innocent face in front of him.

"You know as well as I do how fast she'll go," he answered. "She'll make 18 knots, a little more or less, depending on the sea, wind, and a few tricks."

"I must have more speed," Mohr repeated. "There's got to be some way you can give it to me."

Brinker hesitated. "There is," he replied slowly and reluctantly, "but I don't recommend it."

Mohr's boyish face lit up. "Well?" he demanded, delighted at the prospect of getting what he wanted and clearly ignoring the warning.

"I can connect the electrics to the diesels and run them all together," Brinker told him.

"How long can we run like that?"

"About an hour."

"Fine!" Mohr answered. "Go ahead. If we don't get more speed than this, we'll never catch that convoy in time to sink anything before daylight. An hour ought to do it."

"Aren't you forgetting something?" Brinker asked.

Mohr raised his eyebrows questioningly, and Brinker said, "In an hour running like that, the batteries will be dry. What do you propose to do if a destroyer forces us under?"

Mohr had already turned back to the ladder. He looked at Brinker and grinned. "We'll just have to stay on the surface, won't we?" Then he disappeared up the ladder, calling over his shoulder, "Give me that speed now!"

Brinker stood frowning and thoughtful for a moment. Then he went into the engine room. Mohr would have the speed he wanted.

When Mohr joined his brother grey wolves inside the convoy, the bedlam characteristic of a pack attack was holding sway. The scene could have been taken from Dante's Inferno with the hellish red light from the burning ships casting eerie shadows on the water and the occasional muzzle fire from the escorts flashing as they shot at real or imagined foes. The marauding U-boats raced in and out of the ragged columns firing torpedo after torpedo and dodging the tough escorts. It was a battle to test every ounce of skill and courage and determination of all those involved—whether on merchant ship, escort, or U-boat.

Mohr was a born convoy fighter. He had everything he needed—the soundest of training and the invaluable experience of being Schulz's second-in-command, along with gifts that were harder to pin down, but which were undeniably his. He was smart and bold, and he had luck. He knew when to push his luck past all sensible boundaries, when to gamble everything on a wild chance to stay on the surface, and some inner sense seemed to warn him when his boat was actually spotted.

He had just shot his last torpedo when the destroyer came racing toward him. This time there would be no dodging on the surface, Mohr knew.

"Alarm!"

The bridge watch scrambled frantically down the narrow conning tower to land in a confused heap at the bottom. The boat had already started plunging downward as Mohr jumped through the hatch, slammed the cover, and skidded into the control room.

"Get her down, Brinker!" he yelled, stumbling to his feet. "2A plus 60!"

The slender boat trembled as the electric motors drove her downward at top speed, and she echoed with the sound of running feet as her crew dashed forward to give added weight to the bow.

The boat had just crossed the last column of merchantmen and this destroyer meant business. They could expect depth charges by the dozen and they might be pinned down for a long time.

Suddenly Mohr remembered the batteries and Brinker's warning; the warning he had so confidently chosen to ignore.

"Rolf," he said, his voice low and urgent, "how much juice have we got left?"

"We've got enough, *Capitano*," Brinker told him.

The first string of depth charges went off above them, close enough to shatter the glass covering the gauges in the control room, but not damaging the pressure hull.

Mohr maneuvered his boat delicately and precisely to throw the hunter above him off the scent, but the destroyer captain was skillful and determined, and the patterns of depth charges were terrifyingly close.

Gradually, U-124 was able to put a little distance between herself and her attacker until she could slip quietly away. The depth charges became fewer and farther and at last it was quiet again.

When the boat surfaced, the sea was peaceful and deserted. Dawn was breaking, and the rest of the wolves would be withdrawing now too, licking their wounds and sticking tenaciously to the battered convoy while they waited for another night.

Mohr signaled his report to the admiral, including the fact that he had expended all his torpedoes, along with his estimate of the ships and tonnage they had sunk: 3 tankers, 3 freighters, totaling 44,000 tons, and a probable of 5,000 tons.

This done, he and Brinker sat in the wardroom, enjoying the hot coffee and companionship. They would have to regain contact with the convoy and hold it until released by the BdU, but to all practical purposes, the cruise was over.

Mohr had been waiting for an opportunity to talk to his L.I. since the destroyer had forced them under. It seemed like weeks ago, but Mohr had not forgotten that there were a few answers he wanted from Brinker, and he wanted them privately. He did not waste words on formalities.

"You told me an hour's running with the electric motors coupled to the diesels would take all the juice in the batteries," he said bluntly.

Brinker had been expecting it. "That's right," he answered, unperturbed. "It would have. I disconnected them after half an hour's running."

"What?" Mohr sputtered, completely taken aback. "But you didn't ask permission!"

"You wouldn't have given it," Brinker told him serenely.

"But you . . . you . . . that's *insubordination!*" he stammered, his temper flaring.

"Yes," Brinker answered quietly. "I know."

Mohr stared at him silently for a moment, then his face relaxed in a smile. "You did the right thing, Rolf," he admitted reluctantly. "We did need to keep something in reserve."

The two comrades drank their coffee in quiet and thoughtful companionship.

At last Brinker put his cup down. "Jochen," he said, his use of the commander's first name indicating the close relationship between the two men. "You must listen to your L.I. Engines can do only so much and no more. Some day you may have an L.I. who doesn't have so much experience and doesn't know you so well. He won't be able to stand up against you, but you've got to pay attention to him."

Brinker's face and voice were dead serious. Mohr looked at him thoughtfully. "Yes," he said finally. "You're right, of course. Where would we be now if you hadn't done what you knew was right in spite of me?"

"Signal from the BdU, sir!" The radio operator's head popped through the door. The ill-concealed grin on his face showed that he had read it, and that it was good news.

"Let me have it," Mohr said, reaching out his hand.

He scanned the short wireless message, then threw his head back, roaring with laughter. He handed it over to Brinker, who also burst into howls of glee.

It was the old signal from the captain of the DEUTSCHLAND in answer to the request for Mohr to be detached for special duty. Dönitz had paraphrased it to suit the occasion:

"Der Mohr hat seiner Schuldigkeit getan; der Mohr kann gehen." (Mohr has done his duty; Mohr can go.)

Chapter Nine

THE WAR news was generally good as the U-124 crew went on leave, adding to the buoyant effect of their own successful cruise. German forces were pushing the Russians back along the Eastern front, following the midsummer offensive. Odessa, on the Black Sea, as well as the ancient city of Kiev, had fallen to the Germans, who now launched a frontal drive on Moscow.

There was a disquieting note from the west, however, for Roosevelt on September 11, had announced his "shoot on sight" order to U. S. Naval forces finding Axis vessels west of longitude 26 degrees.

U-124's thorough overhauling had even included a fresh coat of paint for her edelweiss, and she set sail on October 30, 1941, bound for the South Atlantic. Along with U-68 (Merten), U-129 (Bauer), and U-A (Eckermann), U-Mohr formed the Kapstadt Gruppe which would operate around Cape Town.

She carried the same complement of officers as on the previous cruise, plus two more. Dr. Ziemke was the boat's doctor, and Oberleutnant zur See (Ing.) Egon Subklew was making this trip with Brinker before taking over as chief engineering officer on the next cruise.

A few days out of Lorient, some 300 sea miles east of the Azores, Mohr spotted a small fast convoy of two freighters and two destroyers.

He started after it but was unable to make enough speed in the heavy seaway to keep up and soon lost it.

Two days after this he sighted a single-traveling freighter and started closing in to attack. But at twilight the ship, now discernible as a passenger vessel, set her running lights. She also lighted her flag and neutral markings, and Mohr broke off the chase.

Although convoy battles often lasted several days at a time, during which rest and relaxation became merely wistful memories, a U-boat man normally had a great deal of leisure time. Books and cards and never-ending discussions passed the time, and records played over the boat's loud speaker system provided music for additional entertainment.

The universal favorite in U-124's record collection was "Alexander's Ragtime Band," and it had become the traditional accompaniment to any good news or celebration on board.

Long uneventful days at sea were kept from being boring by special entertainments and various contests arranged that involved the whole boat's personnel. And always in the background on U-124 was the happy and incongruous melody of "Alexander's Ragtime Band."

After steaming steadily southward for some three weeks, U-124 met the supply ship PYTHON as planned to top off her fuel tanks before proceeding to South Africa. U-129 was also at the rendezvous, and the three commanders had a chance to exchange news and plans.

Kapitänleutnant Lüders, commander of the PY-THON came aboard the U-124 to speak to Mohr about various supplies required; next day Mohr returned Lüders' call, and also visited Clausen on board U-129.

After leaving the PYTHON, U-124 proceeded southward. On November 22, she received a signal from the BdU to Mohr and Clausen ordering the two boats into their operational areas. Shortly after midnight, another signal from Dönitz came in saying the auxiliary cruiser ATLANTIS, ship 16, had been sunk on November 22.

This plucky ship, under command of the brilliant Kapitän zur See Bernhard Rogge, had roamed the seas, disguising herself as whatever freighter seemed most innocent at the moment, playing wolf in sheep's clothing, and pouncing on unsuspecting merchantmen. She had sunk 22 ships, totaling over 150,000 tons, and had caused untold havoc to the British, who were perpetually being forced to reroute shipping from areas where they suspected her presence.

After a long (622 days) cruise, she had finally been surprised by the British cruiser DEVONSHIRE and sunk. She had been in the process of refueling U-126, and the U-boat was now towing her survivors in life rafts to rendezvous with the PYTHON.

By November 24, U-124 had reached the vicinity of St. Paul's Rocks. Brinker was on the bridge, enjoying a smoke in the warm sunshine and soft breeze. He stood with the bridge watch in companionable silence, the rhythmical throbbing of the diesels soothing to his trained ears as he gazed absently over the sparkling seas around him.

"Ship on the starboard bow!" a lookout reported.

Only the tip of a mast was visible on the horizon, and it was as fine as a needle through the binoculars.

A lookout might search for dozens of hours, in good weather and bad, without seeing a single thing except the vast ocean around him. But if his attention wavered even for a moment, he might miss such a tiny thread of a mast, and thus lose for his boat the chance to attack. Targets were not so plentiful that they could afford to pass one up.

Köster found the mast and watched it grow on the horizon. It was a top mast, and soon the smaller main mast was visible.

"War ship!" he said, not managing to keep the tingle of excitement out of his voice. "Commander to the bridge!"

Mohr soon appeared beside him. "Where? Where?"

She was a warship all right. The tripod masts showed that. Mohr called for full speed on the diesels and set his course to bring him into position to dive and wait for the ship to cross his bow.

As the U-boat roared through the long smooth swells, Mohr established the ship's speed at 18 knots and was able to plot her zig-zag pattern. She was moving on a northwest mean course, zig-zagging in long even legs. Within some forty minutes, he was ready to submerge and lie in wait.

"Clear the bridge," he said. "Make ready to dive." He followed the watch down the hatch. "Dive!"

The boat nosed swiftly down as sea water poured into her diving tanks and her electric motors pushed her, the diving planes determining her angle of descent.

"Take her to 12 meters and level off, L.I.," Mohr said.

He watched through the periscope, observing every detail. "Cruiser," he announced finally. "Let's hope she's not American this time."

Only two days before, they had met another

cruiser, an American of the Memphis class, and had to let her go, furious because they knew she would report them to the British if she saw them. But their orders were explicit: under *no* circumstances were they to attack American ships. The orders made no provision for honest mistakes nor gave any clue as to how to tell the nationality of a blacked-out destroyer zig-zagging around a British convoy. So the exasperated U-boat skippers felt their hands were tied, and cursed the Americans who chased them, held contact on their boats, and guided the Britishers in to attack.

"Look in the Weyer, Zschech," Mohr told the I.WO. "British cruisers."

Zschech read rapidly through the descriptions of the different classes. "Here, Herr Kaleu, what about this?" he said, holding up the book for Mohr to see the silhouette. "British cruisers, Dragon class: H.M.S. DELHI, DESPATCH, DUNEDIN, and DURBAN— two closely spaced funnels, slight rake, after funnel smaller, after fire control placed high, immediately in front of the mainmast, trawler bow."

Mohr nodded. "That's it, then, Dragon class. Make ready all torpedo tubes. We'll shoot in a little while."

Suddenly he heard the sound of breaking glass, followed by spewing water and Brinker's outraged voice, *"Verdammte Scheisse!"*

A gauge above the L.I.'s head had shattered, drenching him and his men with sea water. The boat lurched uncertainly.

"Brinker," Mohr called to him after a moment, "we're on the surface, aren't we?"

"Yes, dammit," snapped Brinker, motioning to his planesmen in front of him, and dismissing the commander from his mind. "Here," he told one of the men, "get below and find the leak in the manometer. Hurry up."

The boat had broached, however briefly, and Mohr knew that if she had been seen, the attack was over before it started. How often did a man get a chance at a shot like that, he wondered impatiently. An enemy cruiser alone, not an escort anywhere to be found, perfect conditions—and his damned boat leaping in the air like a porpoise! He half turned to call to Brinker again. But no, the boat was underwater now. Let the L.I. alone—he already had his hands full if the erratic motion of the boat was any indicator. He did not need the commander to tell him to bring her under control.

Mohr waited a moment longer, then took a quick look through the periscope. The cruiser continued unsuspecting on her course. He stepped back as the periscope slid down in the housing. So she hadn't been seen after all. That was a relief.

"Herr Brinker, I can't move the forward diving planes!"

Brinker grabbed the controls and tugged in vain. "They're jammed," he muttered. "Now what in hell can be the matter with them!"

"Herr Brinker!" came a shout from below. "I found the leak. It's not big."

"Can you cover it with your thumb?" Brinker called back.

"I'll try. But it's pretty strong. I don't know if I can hold it."

"Do the best you can," Brinker told him, turning back to the diving planes controls.

The cruiser and U-boat continued on their respective courses as every minute brought them closer to effective torpedo range. The cruiser followed her zig-zag pattern that Mohr had earlier plotted, her mean course the same. He motioned the periscope up. Another quick look, and suddenly the ship disappeared as an opaque curtain of blue-green Atlantic water covered the periscope lens.

"What's going on down there?" Mohr yelled from the conning tower. "I'm about ready to shoot. Can't you hold the boat steady, Brinker?"

The furious Brinker spun around, swallowing the indignant, profane, and highly insubordinate reply almost on his lips.

"Listen, Captain," he shouted, "the manometer has a leak in it and the forward diving planes are jammed. This boat is goddamned hard to handle!"

"All right, all right, keep your shirt on, Rolf," Mohr told him good-naturedly. "Just do the best you can."

But Brinker wasn't listening to the commander. Having turned back to the controls, he was absorbed in maintaining the delicate balance necessary for an attack, using only the after diving planes and the trimming tanks. It was an almost impossible task, and it was a tribute to Brinker's superb mastery of the boat that she remained steady, ready to fire.

In the conning tower, Mohr raised the periscope for a shooting observation. The horizon was absolutely blank where the cruiser was supposed to be. The startled Mohr glanced up in momentary confusion and brushed the back of his hand across his eyes. How could she have utterly disappeared? After all the trouble trimming the boat, now was the damned cruiser bewitched? He walked around the periscope, searching the full circle of the horizon. At last he found her, off to port, and long gone.

He swore angrily. After more than two hours of zig-zags as regular as clockwork, the wretched cruiser had suddenly changed course. Now she was already out of range. Or was she?

It was an impossible shot, obviously. But Mohr was at his best in impossible situations. Now he called out a new set of figures to the torpedo mixers as he quickly calculated the cruiser's range and angle on the bow. He would have to assume she was holding the same speed.

Three torpedoes left the tubes, and Zschech set the stop watch.

In the control room below, Brinker, soaked with sweat, fought like a madman to keep the boat from broaching with the sudden loss of weight in the bow as the fish were fired. Hampered by the loss of the forward diving planes, he quickly flooded the bow tanks and only just managed to keep her nose down.

Throughout the boat, the men stood motionless, concentrating on the three long slim torpedoes gliding through the water.

"Still running?" Mohr asked with his eyes, nodding toward the hydrophone operator.

He nodded back in the affirmative.

Zschech looked at the stop watch in his hand. Two minutes running time. Two and a half.

The men looked at each other. If they hadn't hit by now, they wouldn't. Might as well fire another spread or forget her. Those fish were already well past the usual running time for a shot.

Three minutes.

"Hard port," Mohr said. "Come to 70 degrees. We'll give her a stern shot. Make ready tubes 5 and 6."

But still his attention was centered on the three fish still running, and he occasionally glanced at the stop watch in Zschech's hand.

Four and a half minutes. Five minutes.

"Up scope," Mohr's voice broke the tense silence in the conning tower.

The men close beside him watched him intently. Was there still any hope that the shot would hit? The Old Man seemed to think so.

Suddenly Mohr's body stiffened. His fists grasped the periscope handles tightly, and he cried out, "Oh, it's sunk!"

He watched hypnotized as the water rained down around the ship, hiding her. Then as the geyser from the explosion cleared away, he could see her again, and he said, "No, no . . . she's hit, but still afloat."

He had not moved at the periscope. "Hit!" he shouted. "The second torpedo has hit!"

This time the detonation was followed by a tremendous internal explosion that gutted the cruiser. Almost immediately, she rolled heavily over on her side, her funnels almost touching the water toward the U-boat like some monstrous sea creature in the throes of violent death. Then she rolled to the other side, righted herself briefly, and sank, stern first.

Mohr had hit her with two out of three shots from the incredible range of over three miles. It took 5 minutes 23 seconds running time for the torpedoes to reach her.

He sent the brief signal to Dönitz: "Sunk English cruiser D Class."

Three hours later Dönitz's joking praise came back to this favorite commander: *"Der Mohr had seine Schuldigkeit getan!"*

As soon as the attack was finished, Brinker set about to repair the forward diving planes and found they were jammed by a piece of rope someone had forgotten to remove. There had been no damage to them.

Arriving at zero latitude next day, U-124 ignored the war and bowed to tradition as she paid homage to King Neptune in the universal shipboard ceremonies of crossing the line.

It was brought to Commander Mohr's attention that some of those on board his vessel belonged to

that wretched category of Lowly Pollywogs, and that
His Majesty King Neptune, Ruler of the Deep, would
shortly appear on board in person to remedy the
situation.

There was a carnival air on board as those who had
already attained the status of Ancient Shellback prepared to initiate those Pollywogs who were crossing the equator for the first time. Huge pills were
created in the galley by Neptune's fiendish helpers
who gleefully combined salt and other kitchen staples
with a liberal dose of diesel oil from the engine room.

Subklew, resplendent in flowing beard, wearing a
crown and carrying a trident, solemnly announced
himself as King Neptune and ordered Mohr to turn
out the crew.

They lined up on the upper deck, laughing while
their skipper humbly took orders from this wild ap-
parition from the deep who had taken over the boat
and was now proceeding to hold court in the rowdy
and traditional manner of sailors everywhere.

Lowly Pollywogs were hauled before His Majesty,
made to confess their crime, and heard their sentence
pronounced. They swallowed the nauseating pills and
had their bodies smeared with grease and dirt, then
were commanded to run around the conning tower
for several laps. As a final indignity, they were
sprayed with the hose, after which they were declared to be Ancient Shellbacks.

But it was dangerous to have so many men on deck
at the time, and the war, although it might have been
momentarily forgotten by the laughing men taking
part in the ridiculous rites, was not really very far
away. The lookouts on the bridge, keeping sharp
watch on the sky and the distant horizon, dared not
relax their vigil even for a second as their comrades
depended on them for safety.

The ceremonies were short, lasting only fifteen or twenty minutes. But U-124, like countless other ships, both Allied and German, had paid her homage to King Neptune. As on the other ships, the duties and dangers of war would have to wait, or at least share their priority, while their crews momentarily joined hands with all sailors everywhere in their own special heritage.

At 1455 on the morning of December 2, U-124 intercepted a signal from U-Merten to the BdU saying that PYTHON, which had been the refuge of the ATLANTIS' shipwrecked crew, had herself fallen victim to a British cruiser, coincidentally the DORSETSHIRE, sister ship to the DEVONSHIRE.

Eckermann, also at the scene, added details in a signal to Dönitz minutes later, and the two boats reported no losses among the combined raider crews. The U-boats had managed to get the men into lifeboats and had them in tow.

Dönitz signaled Mohr and Clausen to report their positions and remaining fuel and provisions.

Mohr replied, "Marinequadrat F T 83. 112 cbm. Mohr."

By early morning of December 3, the rescue operation was well under way. Rogge, as senior officer, was in command at the scene; and Dönitz, at his headquarters, after receiving full reports from all his boats in the area, had ordered the Kapstadt group into the rescue.

En route, U-124 spotted a freighter, and Mohr took up the chase. He followed the ship through the afternoon, puzzling over her identity. She flew no flag, which indicated that she was not neutral. By dark U-124 was in shooting position and waiting. When the ship failed to set running lights, Mohr torpedoed her.

Three torpedoes hit; one under the forward mast,

one under the after mast, and one in the engine room sent her to the bottom.

Several lifeboats were launched, and Mohr hailed one to ask her identity. The captain of the sunk ship indignantly informed him that she was the American SAGADAHOC, bound for Durban out of New York with general cargo.

Mohr apologized, and was answered only by outraged silence. When he asked if he might give the survivors any provisions, they told him they had everything, and set their sails and left.

"They'll have plenty to tell the world about us 'U-boat Butchers' now, you can be sure," Köster said as they watched the Americans disappear.

Mohr grinned at him ruefully. "And nothing on earth could convince him we'd never have touched him if he'd just turned on his damned running lights."

"Well, if he's going around disguised as a Britisher, he can expect to get sunk like one!"

"That's true," Mohr agreed. "All the same, I wish the bastard could be in my shoes when I have to tell Uncle Karl about this little error."

With this grim confrontation in mind, Mohr noted in his log that he had acted entirely in accordance with Standing War Order No. 105, section C. He then signaled Dönitz that he had sunk the U.S. ship SAGADAHOC and that she was blacked out and carried no neutral markings.

Mohr again set his course to meet U-A and the raider survivors, but on arrival at his estimated point of interception, the sea around him was quite empty. He combed the area, shooting signal flares at intervals, until it became plain there had been a major error in somebody's plots.

He signaled Dönitz asking for a fix from one of the

rescue boats. Dönitz relayed the message to Eckermann and Merten to guide Mohr in.

Eckermann signaled his position to Mohr shortly
afterward, and it was apparent that the two boats
had passed each other about 9 miles apart at 7 o'clock
the previous morning. Mohr turned back to follow the
new heading to U-A, which began sending signals at
regular intervals.

That afternoon, U-124 again passed the spot where
she had sunk the SAGADAHOC, still coated with oil
and littered with wreckage. Six drums of transmission
oil were spotted and hauled aboard, along with a
drum of ball bearing lubricant and 18 canisters of oil.
The engineers received them only too thankfully
since oil had become a problem on this cruise.

Some of the oil taken on in Lorient had been
sabotaged and was unusable, creating a serious shortage. Finding these drums intact was like a gift from
King Neptune himself.

It was not, however, quite a gift, and Mohr well
knew it. Sinking an American ship was a serious
matter, and he knew Dönitz would be furious. Facing
the admiral in such a mood was something even the
most reckless officer would prefer to avoid. So Mohr
was, in a way, buying the oil they needed so badly,
and he was not at all satisfied with the price he knew
he would have to pay.

The sea around them was now almost covered with
automobile tires. The men on the deck fished two out
of the water and took them to the bridge where they
were claimed as trophies.

Along with the tires, there were thousands of baby
shoes floating incongruously in the debris. One of the
men picked up a few at random, then called out, "Hey
look! I've found a pair and I think they'll fit my
baby!"

A lasting souvenir of the unhappy freighter was her name, which the U-124 crew adopted as a recognition signal. While on leave, when any of the crew met each other, no matter where, they would shout "SAGADAHOC — SAGADAHOC — SAGADAHOC!" like a football cheer.

His mind still on Dönitz, Mohr shrugged and went below. The Big Lion would chew him up when he got back to base—harsh punishments were part of the game when one disobeyed orders, and commanders were not exempt. Fritz Lemp had spent his precious leave confined to quarters studying foreign ship silhouettes following what was an honest mistake on his part, Mohr reflected. But there was not much point in worrying about it now. The time would come soon enough. Brinker was later kind enough to remind him that if they got sunk he would not have to face Dönitz at all.

"Alexander's Ragtime Band" was put on the record player, and U-124 resumed her course to the other U-boats and the raider survivors. And despite his apprehension, Mohr was to be saved from the admiral's wrath by an event that more than adequately obscured his own indiscretion. This was December 3, 1941. Four days later, the Japanese attacked Pearl Harbor.

It was still dark on the morning of December 5, when U-124 joined the bedraggled little German armada. The other U-boats had taken aboard all the men they could carry, and were towing the rest in life boats. They were tied up together in the gentle swells waiting Mohr's arrival, the lifeboats lashed between them to act as fenders.

U-124 pulled alongside U-68, and Mohr, high-spirited and gay, scampered across the lifeboats to climb up on the bridge of U-68. He greeted his fellow officers there, slapping them on the back as casually and unconcerned as though they had all met in a favorite bar.

One of the officers thus greeted was Kapitän Rogge, and he failed to be charmed by Mohr's conviviality. Still shocked and grieved by the loss of his ship, his impatience was understandable as every passing hour in the rendezvous point brought not only more discomfort to all of them, but increased their danger as well.

Mohr explained that he had been delayed partly on account of incorrect position reports, as well as the fact that for awhile he and Eckermann were using different wave lengths. There was a further delay on account of the ship he had chased and sunk, and this, along with the chummy slap on the back was the final straw for Rogge's frazzled nerves and patience.

A stinging reprimand from the angry four-striper, however, left Mohr unmoved and unrepentant. He had been sent out to sink ships and sink ships he would. And if it meant his countrymen had to spend an extra night in a raft, then so be it. His reply was a polite and non-committal, "Aye, aye, sir."

Still miffed over Mohr's casual greeting, Rogge was later heard to remark, "Present-day naval officers have no manners."

Before setting out on independent courses for France, U-68 gave 50 cbm. diesel fuel and 1000 liters lubricating oil to U-124, along with 6 officers and 98 petty officers and men from Ship 16. There were now 104 extra men stuffed into a U-boat built to accommodate a crew of 48 thoroughly crowded and uncomfortable officers and men. And the men who sailed under the edelweiss now shared their bunks with not one, but several others, and watched the exhausted survivors take turns standing, sitting, and lying down.

The U-boat men, accustomed to their cramped quarters and stifling atmosphere, could not help admiring the fortitude of their passengers who, along with their other miseries, had to cope with varying degrees of claustrophobia.

Shortly after 1200 on December 9, U-124 came in sight of Ascension Island. Visibility was excellent, and a light breeze played over the short swells.

Mohr stood on the bridge, silently watching the British base. Suddenly he turned, ordered a change of course, and clattered down the ladder into the control room.

The thoughtful commander on the bridge was now the irrepressible and invincible skipper with the golden touch, for whom the most wildly improbable and reckless ventures invariably succeeded.

Brinker, grinning, joined the watch officers as Mohr, laughing and gesturing, outlined his plan. It seemed such a waste to creep unnoticed by the British port of Georgetown, and it was Mohr's contention that, aside from the ships he might be able to sink in the harbor, his presence, if detected, would be a disruptive force in itself. Since he was the last German boat to leave the South Atlantic, it would be advantageous to alarm the British into fruitless hunts for U-boats that had already gone.

Mohr's crew, as always, was caught up in his excitement and spirit. "Our Mohr has luck," they would say. And projects that might have been regarded with alarm as near-suicide on another boat were tackled with abandon on Mohr's.

With her 104 involuntary passengers literally packed inside like sardines in a can, attacking conditions on board U-124 were scarcely ideal. But the boat still handled well, and Brinker could dive and trim her with no difficulty.

If the hapless passengers might have preferred going straight home to joining a raid on a well-defended British port, their preference had just dropped to a very low priority when Mohr's plan was announced.

Mohr, curiosity completely overruling caution, headed his boat on the surface within six miles of Georgetown, but much to his disgust, the harbor was empty. The harbor's inhabitants were not asleep, however, and they plainly resented a German U-boat's invasion of a British port. By way of expressing their sentiments, they opened up with the shore batteries at Fort Thornton, and the shells were soon falling uncomfortably close to the nosy and uninvited guest.

Hans Köster announced with some indignation, "They're shooting at us!" Just as Mohr arrived at the same conclusion.

U-124 crash-dived, beating an undignified retreat, and surfaced some distance away, well out of range of the inhospitable Fort Thornton guns.

"Herr Kaleu," Schroeder called. "I've picked up the shore station at Ascension."

Mohr held the earphone to his ear and listened attentively. Over and over the alarm was given: "German submarine sighted at Fort Thornton."

British destroyers in the vicinity picked up the signal, and soon the air was full of their signals crackling back and forth with the short station and among themselves.

Mohr listened, his grey eyes twinkling with delight at the agitation and alarm he had brought about. Then, with a broad grin, he sent his own message out on the British wave length: "Position please."

There was instant radio silence.

Having achieved the commotion Mohr had hoped

for, if not any actual sinkings, U-124 again turned
northward toward France.

With the added drain on the air supply inside the
boat due to the large number of men on board, the
air was so foul as to be almost unbreathable. Food
and water were in seriously short supply.

The boat had been scheduled to be supplied from
PYTHON within the next few days, and was low on
provisions even before taking on the survivors. Of
more immediate concern to Brinker, however, was
the desperate shortage of lubricating oil. He gave
Mohr the disquieting news that they could not get
home on what they had.

Assuming command at headquarters for the rescue
operation, Dönitz had contacted the Flag Officer of
Italian Submarines and got four boats. These were
ordered to rendezvous with the German boats, which,
after dividing up their fuel oil, were making for their
bases independently.

U-124 again crossed the equator on the night of
December 11, and at midnight she received a message from Dönitz announcing that Brinker had been
awarded the German Cross in Gold. This time he was
decorated in recognition of his superb control of the
boat under extremely adverse conditions that had
made possible the sinking of the DUNEDIN.

Mohr had already been informed that the Italian
boat CALVI would bring them not only food and
water, but also the essential lubricating oil.

Due to the almost completely exhausted supply of
this oil, U-124 made it to her rendezvous point on one
diesel. When dawn brought no sign of the Italian
boat, Mohr fired a star shell. There was no reply, and
he cruised around the area throughout the day searching.

When darkness came, with still no sign of the CAL-

VI, he lay with engines stopped through the night to conserve oil. At daylight he resumed his search at slow speed, and fired another star shell. At 1249, the CALVI came in sight.

The Italians pulled alongside, and with smiles, good humor, and what seemed to the Germans an incredible amount of confusion, proceeded to dispense the provisions they had brought and take on 70 of the survivors. During this time, Mohr visited the captain, Lt.Cdr. Olivieri, on board the CALVI.

Brinker waited impatiently. Finally he asked the Italian chief engineer, "Where's the lubricating oil?"

"Lubricating oil?" asked the Italian, raising his eyebrows. "But we've brought you diesel oil!"

"We've got diesel oil," Brinker told him. "You were supposed to bring lubricating oil."

"We only have lubricating oil for our own use," the Italian informed him placidly. "We brought you diesel oil."

"We've got to have lubricating oil or we can't get home!" shouted Brinker, at his wit's end.

The Italian officers called for a pow-wow and discussed the matter at length while Brinker pleaded humbly for the oil one minute, then losing his temper the next, arrogantly demanded it.

At last they agreed to give him 1,000 liters, and not a drop more. Since there was not enough of this suddenly priceless commodity to supply both boats, they ruled that it would not be the CALVI caught short. Brinker, not at all agreeing with their decision, had no choice but to accept his 1,000 liters and limp back to France on one diesel.

Christmas Day, for the second time, found U-124 still at sea, and her crew and their guests celebrated as best they could. Matrosen Obergefreiter Laubisch, a very big and calm man, put his talented hands to work and made a tree out of wire and green paper. Cigarette papers and tin foil were fashioned into ornaments for it, and the little boat rang with familiar Christmas carols.

A signal arrived from Dönitz to all U-boats at sea: "On German Christmas, I am with heart and thoughts with you, my proud, hard-fighting U-boat crews."

U-124 arrived at St. Nazaire on December 29, the last of the rescue boats. She flew the pennants, also made by Laubisch, which told the ships she had sunk, and a tire from the luckless SAGADAHOC was hung on her cannon barrel.

Four hundred fourteen survivors of the combined ATLANTIS and PYTHON crews had been brought back to the Biscay bases by 8 sumarines from a distance of 5,000 miles of enemy-held waters. The most far-reaching rescue operation of the war had succeeded without the loss of a single man.

When U-124 tied up at her pier, there was a special little delegation to greet Brinker. Having held onto her lubricating oil and thus having the use of two diesels instead of one, the CALVI had reached port well ahead of U-124. Now her officers came aboard, and ceremoniously presented Brinker with a drink.

Brinker took the glass and raised it in a salute to the smiling Italian officers. As he looked into the clear white liquid, it seemed to have a peculiarly familiar consistency, and his eyes narrowed slightly. He nodded to his guests, smiled with his lips and cursed them in his heart, then he raised the glass and slowly, with feigned enjoyment, he drained it.

His suspicions had been well-founded. The Italians, in deference to his ruffled feathers over the lubricating oil, had given him a glass of pure castor oil.

They stared astonished at this display of German

guts as Brinker emptied the glass, and handed it back to them.

"That was delicious," he informed them, smiling. "May I please have another glass?"

The Italians burst out laughing and hugged Brinker delightedly. "Try this," they said, bringing out a bottle of cognac. "It's even better!"

Chapter Ten

WITH THE Japanese attack on Pearl Harbor, the
United States had now entered the fray officially.
The "threat from the west" so dreaded by the German Military was no longer threat, but reality. The
limitless potential of industry and agriculture, as well
as manpower, that was the United States was now
wholly committed on the side of the Allies. There
remained only the problem of transporting this vast
complex of war material across the Atlantic Ocean.
And preventing it was Dönitz's department.

But once again, the outbreak of war caught him
short and unawares. The Japanese attack was as
much a surprise to the Germans as it was to the
Americans, and boats which Dönitz could have sta-
tioned in strategic positions were scattered far and
wide, in dry docks, en route to and from operational
areas. He was prevented by higher authority from
taking any of the 23 boats from the Mediterranean or
the 4 each in the Gibraltar and Norwegian areas, so
only 5 boats could be made ready to depart from the
Biscay bases between December 16 and 25. It was
with this modest number that he launched his over-

whelmingly successful offensive, Operation Paukenschlag.

For the U-boat men themselves, the declaration of war on December 11, was in a way a relief. At least the shadow war in the Atlantic was over. Dönitz's orders to his commanders had been simple and to the point. Incidents with the United States were to be avoided at all costs. Under *no* circumstances were they to attack American ships, merchant or warships, not even in self-defense.

Commanders and crews who had sweated out depth charge attacks by teams of British and American destroyers now itched to get an "Ami" in their sights. Revenge would be sweet.

Reports of success by the Paukenschlag boats soon came back to headquarters. Reinhard Hardegen in U-123 reported 8 ships sunk with a tonnage of 53,360 tons: Korvettenkapitän Zapp (U-66) sank 5 with 50,000 tons; and Korvettenkapitän Kals (U-130) sank 4 with 30,748 tons. The other boats reported similarly high success, and a large percentage of this tonnage was tankers, a particularly valuable prize.

The American coast was the plum assignment now for a U-boat, so Mohr was of course delighted to find that his next operational area would be what had quickly become known as the "Golden West." Furthermore, he was given "free hunting" and not restricted to any one area.

Eager to learn all he could about conditions in the new combat zone, he talked by the hour to commanders who had just returned, storing up every scrap of information that might be useful to him.

First of all, he was told, the American coast was lit up with cities, beacons, lighthouses, and such, making it easy to see ships silhouetted against the coast line. Not only that, but the ships carried their normal running lights. In case he would like to plan his attacks systematically, all he had to do was tune in the American radio, since departures and arrivals were broadcast and merchant ships also regularly reported their own positions. In addition to this, the schedules of anti-submarine patrols by aircraft and destroyers were broadcast and followed most accurately. Zapp assured him that he would be able to set his watch by their punctuality.

The inexperienced American ASW crews were no match for the wily Germans who were used to the tenacious British escorts. For a year and a half these two old adversaries had matched skill for skill in a battle that was as harsh and unrelenting as the North Atlantic itself. The Americans were new to the game. But they would learn.

While this bonanza lasted, the Germans were determined to make the most of it. U-124 was a Type IX B, and the western Atlantic was well within her cruising range, allowing for a stay of several weeks. The Type VII C's, smaller and with correspondingly less cruising radius, were also thrown into the attack, their enterprising commanders and crews having taken matters into their own hands concerning their capacity for fuel and stores. Normally crowded beyond all reasonable bounds at the beginning of a cruise, they now took on tons of extra stores, even stacking them in bunks, and sacrificing some of their meager fresh water bunkers for diesel oil.

U-373, one of the VII C's so determined not to miss out where targets were plentiful and destroyers few, had thus clandestinely equipped herself for an extended cruise. Upon reaching her assigned battle area off the Newfoundland Banks, her Commander Loeser signaled headquarters the amount of fuel and provisions he had left, and asked permission to go on to the

U.S. coast. A week later this boat rounded Cape May and brazenly entered Delaware Bay to lay mines under the very nose of an American destroyer.

Korvettenkapitän Victor Schütze, chief of the 2nd U-Flotilla, told his commanders to load up with everything they had, including gear for all seasons and climates. These boats quickly earned the nicknames of "Woolworth's at Sea" and the "Great German Underwater Warehouse."

And in spite of the long distances involved, targets so abounded and attacking conditions were so favorable that torpedoes were expended long before the fuel situation would have forced them to start for home. Small wonder the U-boat men called it the "American Shooting Season!"

Commander Zapp had suggested to Mohr that he try the waters around Cape Hatteras, traditional graveyard of ships with its shallow waters and bad weather. Merchant ships followed the peacetime shipping routes, and it should be an ideal spot for a prowling U-boat. These treacherous waters that had already claimed so many ships through the years would find 400 more victims during the war, mostly from German U-boats.

Brinker was gone from the boat. Having been with her since before her launching in Bremen, he had been aboard longer and known her better than any other man, and he could not leave without regrets. But few chief engineers had made as many as 11 war cruises, as had Brinker, and his knowledge and experience were invaluable. Now he would serve as flotilla chief engineering officer. With Mohr as commander, and Subklew as L.I., U-124 was in good and capable hands.

Hans Köster had been promoted from second to first watch officer, and Peter Zschech had been transferred off. He would shortly receive his own command, U-505, and would die by his own hand before the war was over.

U-124 left Lorient on February 21, heading west on her most economical cruising speed. It would take some three weeks to reach her destination, for Mohr had followed Zapp's advice and chosen Cape Hatteras.

Mohr and his crew were in a holiday mood, and the U-124 rang with laughter, songs, and the ever-present "Alexander's Ragtime Band." Mohr had carefully selected a library for his boat, and during the long trip, the men read and talked about the books together. These discussions, planned by the commander to help fight boredom in the crew, soon grew into lively and witty affairs.

He had also brought books for himself, leaving another copy of them at home for his wife. Thus they would read the same books while he was on patrol, and it somehow shortened the thousands of miles between them until his next leave when they could be together again.

His leaves were somewhat quieter affairs for Mohr since his marriage, each day spent with his wife and friends immeasurably precious to him. The luxury of sleeping the mornings away uninterrupted and then spending the rest of the day and far into the night doing anything he pleased, as he pleased, was a blissful contrast to the heavy responsibilities of command.

Once before the war, while he was Admiral Marschall's flag lieutenant, he had spent a considerably wilder leave, notable for two brushes with the law. First, he and some friends, in the middle of a party at the beach, spied a piano on a nearby porch and proceeded to requisition it. Mohr, an excellent pianist, played while the others danced and sang—that is, until the police appeared.

They were all carted off to the local police station, where their names were duly registered, and the policeman in charge, remarking that Mohr was the ringleader and the worst of all, asked his occupation. When Mohr told him he was an Oberleutnant in the navy, the indignant policeman said, "But you're behaving like a little boy! You should be ashamed of yourself!"

Called on the carpet before Admiral Marschall when he returned, he was sternly told, "I have two letters from the police regarding you. One about the piano escapade, and the other one tells me that you and seven other boys piled into a four-passenger car and drove down the sidewalks chasing pedestrians! Now what have you to say for yourself?"

"Yes, it's true. I did it," Mohr freely admitted.

Admiral Marschall shook his head. "Ah, you are a devil!" he muttered. Then he smiled. "But you are young, and I like you, so, I tear up the letter."

But before the young flag lieutenant was dismissed, he was given to understand that it would be well to see to it that such "Affentheater" was never again brought to the admiral's attention.

Since that narrow squeak, Mohr had prudently seen to it that all "monkey business" escaped the attention of his commanding officers. But his keen wit and playful disposition remained as irrepressible as ever, to the constant delight of his crew. And long though the voyage from Lorient to the Carolina coast was, it was not dull.

On March 14, U-124 had gotten as far west as Bermuda when she made contact with another ship.

"Ship on the starboard bow!"

The lookout's cry rang through the boat, and with

it, the electric excitement of going in to the attack. U-124 was cocked and primed.

"Hard starboard!" Mohr called through the speaking tube. "Full speed on both diesels!"

It was a bright clear afternoon with good visibility, and Mohr began circling around the ship to reach his firing position. Matching his speed to hers for a short time gave him an accurate estimate of her speed for the torpedo settings.

The ship, a medium-sized tanker, was loaded and deep in the water. She was zig-zagging with short regular zags, and the U-boat, now ahead of her, dived to lie in wait on her base course line. It was now twilight.

Mohr had sent the firing data to fire control, where the torpedo settings were calculated and duly passed on to the mixers.

"Torpedo one and two . . . los!"

The first torpedo hit the after part of the forecastle and the second hit under the forward mast. The bow of the ship went suddenly deeper into the water as though she would sink, then she lay quite still in the water.

Mohr watched as a lifeboat was launched from the port side, and he carefully observed details of the tanker. He could see three guns, probably about 5 cm., and what appeared to be a 10.5 cm. or 15 cm. gun on the stern. This one was manned and began firing in the direction of the periscope.

"We'll fire another one," Mohr said. "She's not sinking."

He called out the settings and watched through the sights as the tanker came into the cross hairs.

"Torpedo . . . los!"

The third torpedo hit between the after mast and engine room, and the magazine exploded into a ball of flame that engulfed the ship. Burning oil spread out around her, turning the sea into a carpet of fire.

Mohr brought the boat to the surface, and the men on the bridge watched silently, their faces grim in the horrible glare from the burning ship. Flames shot 200 meters into the air, and smoke billowed up 800 meters high. More ammunition exploded at intervals as the ship burned furiously.

"Both diesels ahead slow," Mohr finally said, breaking the spell they had felt themselves under watching the wild flames leaping into the now dark sky. "We'll try to get close enough to make out her name."

The U-boat moved slowly toward the appalling scene in front of them, but was soon forced to turn away from the searing heat. The tanker floated in a sea of burning oil.

As Köster watched the blazing ship, he could see a lifeboat and two rafts close by her, the rescue craft afire like the doomed ship they had tried to escape. There were four small dots in the water a little further out, and he watched them, puzzled for a second. Then with a shock of horror, he realized they were men, swimming in a hopeless attempt to save themselves. The sweat on his face and body was suddenly like ice water, and he felt himself choking with revulsion.

Klein, also watching the nightmare of flames in front of him, saw the swimming men, and turned away shuddering. "Dear God," he thought, "where do they find a man who will go to sea on a tanker?"

"There," Mohr murmured, "I can make it out now. She's the BRITISH RESOURCE—London."

The U-boat continued her voyage west, the glow from the burning oil lighting the sky behind them until nearly dawn.

A small freighter crossed the U-boat's path east of

Hatteras on March 12. Mohr fired one torpedo in a surfaced attack, and the ship sank within three minutes. She did not wireless.

The U-boat approached the ship's survivors, who had launched two lifeboats and several floats. They told Mohr that she was the CEIBA, bound from Jamaica to New York with a cargo of bananas.

Leaving the survivors, U-124 again turned westward. By dawn, she had passed the 200 meter line and was steering for the 40-meter line off Diamond Shoals when Mohr spotted a ship, directly in front of him, about four sea miles away. He dived, and let the four-masted schooner pass within 600 meters of him. He decided the 300-ton ship was not worth a torpedo, and the rough sea made an attack with the deck guns impossible. So he watched her sail away as he put his boat into position to intercept ships in the regular traffic lanes.

He had not long to wait before the lookouts found a ship in ballast, heading south. Mohr sank the small freighter, attacking on the surface and firing one torpedo from a bow tube.

He dodged the destroyer that came close by, then turned back to attack a second freighter, also moving southward. He fired a bow shot from a distance of 400 meters, which hit midships, just under her stack, and the ship turned off to port.

A plane forced U-124 under, and dropped a bomb close by. The dull rumble of depth charges could be heard in the distance as the boat moved out to the 100-meter line to reload her tubes.

When she came back to the surface, U-124 sighted another ship, and turned to attack. She was the 6,878 ton tanker ACME, under the command of Captain Sigismund Schulz, en route in ballast from New York to Corpus Christi, Texas.

In addition to the U-boat stalking her, which she could not see, she had plenty of visible company. The Greek tanker KASSANDRA LOULOUDIS and two other ships were astern, the tanker also headed south; and ahead two tankers and two freighters were in sight. The destroyer USS DICKERSON and the Coast Guard cutter DIONE were also within four miles of her.

At 5:50, local time, a torpedo exploding beneath the engine room rocked the ACME, blasting a hole 30 to 40 feet in diameter in her hull, and killing eleven men who were in the engine room and crew's quarters just abaft. Half an hour later, the survivors abandoned ship, and within 10 minutes were picked up by the DIONE.

A speeding destroyer passed within 1.25 miles of the U-124 without seeing the boat. Mohr estimated her to be a Campbell Type, and decided she must be patrolling the 20-meter line. U-124, still undetected, had cautiously pulled back a little toward deeper water. The place was crawling with ships.

So far it had been almost too easy. But Mohr did not let himself be deceived; should he be discovered and attacked in a mere 20 meters of water, he scarcely stood a prayer. He did not have the speed to outrun a destroyer, and in waters too shallow to dive, he could not hope to escape even the most inexperienced submarine hunter.

No one followed, so Mohr turned his boat toward the tanker KASSANDRA LOULOUDIS, which was astern the ACME. He came in close and fired two torpedoes. Both hit at 7:15, and the tanker sank a short time later.

As the boat turned back away from land, a lookout called out, "Destroyer!"

"Full speed!" Mohr yelled. "Twice full speed!"

They had to reach deeper water in order to dive. "Clear the bridge!"

As soon as enough depth registered under her hull, U-124 headed down—and not a moment too soon, for a seaplane had spotted them and dropped a bomb or depth charge. It rocked the whole boat, breaking glass and rattling her crew around like dice in a cup. There was no damage to the hull, but it had been close.

A few minutes later, the U-boat's crew could hear a pattern of depth charges exploding in the distance. They looked at each other questioningly. Were they meant for us? Then they smiled. If they were, then the Amis had better improve their aim.

With the dawn, U-124 pulled out to about the 60-meter line and lay on the bottom, her engines stopped. This was the routine she would follow throughout the cruise, submerged most of the day to conserve fuel and let her crew sleep, and hunting on the surface close inshore by night.

The following night, U-124 returned to her hunting grounds along the 20-meter line, Mohr still marveling at the brightly lit Lookout Lighthouse and the radio beacons from Lookout and Charleston impartially guiding friend and foe alike.

A ship came in sight just south of Cape Lookout, and Mohr circled around ahead of her as he made his firing calculations. It was a dark clear night, with winds gentle to moderate. The sea was choppy, but not too rough. He couldn't have asked for better conditions.

"Target speed 11.5 knots," Mohr said. "Course 236 degrees true."

At 9:30 he fired his first torpedo, which hit aft on the port side.

The ship was the SS PAPOOSE, a 5,939 gross ton

tanker, sailing in ballast from Providence, Rhode Island, bound for Corpus Christi.

She was thrown into sudden confusion as the torpedo ripped into her port side, penetrating a fuel tank and tearing interior bulkheads. Oil and water poured into the engine room, and within four minutes had risen as high as the tops of the cylinder heads. The ship's engine, disabled by the torpedo, stopped immediately.

The merchant sailors, unused to war, but long trained in the sea's ways, reacted to sudden danger with speed and certainty.

Third mate R. M. Wenning was standing bridge watch on the PAPOOSE. When the torpedo hit, stopping her engine, he instantly ordered the wheel put hard starboard in an effort to turn her toward shore. But she had only turned about two degrees off her course when she lost headway completely and lay dead in the water.

As soon as the torpedo hit, the radio operator, F. K. Russell, had sent out SOS, repeated three times, and the following signal: "SSSS—WNBS—SS PA-POOSE—Position 15 miles SW Cape Lookout." It was promptly acknowledged.

PAPOOSE was still afloat, but Captain Zalnic realized she would probably not be for long. The U-boat that had fired the first torpedo would no doubt shoot another one. At least he could get his crew off. He ordered them to abandon ship, and the first lifeboat was launched five minutes after the attack.

Captain Zalnic had been right in expecting a second attack. U-124 had already circled around the bow of the stopped ship to observe.

"It will take another fish to sink her," Mohr decided. "And be quick about it," he added, turning to the I.WO. "We're on the land side of her, and we'd have more water under us in a bathtub than we've got here."

"Herr Kaleu!" the radio man called. "Ship is the SS PAPOOSE. She just wirelessed an SOS."

"Did a shore station acknowledge?" Mohr called back.

"Yes!"

"Very well," Mohr said, turning back to Köster. "We'd better sink her quick and get out of here while we still can."

The tanker's crew was following Captain Zalnic's order to abandon ship, and the men on the first lifeboat were already rowing away from the ship. Suddenly a long dark shape streaked through the water, passing within a foot of the lifeboat.

The scream, "Torpedo!" electrified the men on the deck of the PAPOOSE, and they watched helplessly as the torpedo track, about 50 feet away on the starboard quarter, came straight at them. It hit aft of midships, tearing a huge jagged hole in the hull, partly above the water line.

Within five minutes after the second hit, the second lifeboat was launched. Falling debris had caused the after fall of the lifeboat to foul when the boat was still some 15 feet above the water. Captain Zalnic ordered the bow lowered and he cut the after fall. The lifeboat was then quickly rowed away from the ship.

U-124, meantime, had wheeled around the ship and was now making for open water. Her crew could all breathe easier with a safe depth under her hull.

As the boat turned southwestward, the lookouts sighted another tanker, loaded, on a reciprocal course to them. Within 10 minutes, Mohr had put his boat into position for a two-torpedo shot with the bow tubes.

The first torpedo hit abaft the forecastle, sending shock waves of sound to the U-boat, 800 meters away. The second torpedo missed.

The tanker, the E. H. HUTTON, was slowly settling in the water, and she radioed a distress signal on the 600-meter band. Eight minutes later, Mohr shot a third torpedo, which hit under the bridge. The bow dipped under the water, and flames suddenly covered the tanker's bridge as the U-boat turned and headed south. For three-quarters of an hour the U-boat's bridge watch could see the bright glow from the burning ship. Then suddenly it vanished. The ship had sunk.

Cape Hatteras was living up to their expectations, and U-124's success climbed with each night. Merchant ships were traveling as close inshore as they dared, apparently hoping that U-boats would not venture into such shallow waters. At least some of them were unaware that these night attacks were generally delivered on the surface, so the lack of depth became a real danger to U-boats only if they were themselves attacked. This was a risk their commanders were willing to assume, so they required no more depth than the merchantmen.

Just past midnight on March 21, U-124 headed southward toward Frying Pan Buoy. The wind was light, but heavy rain showers pelted the men on the bridge and all but blinded them. Even when the rain stopped at intervals, visibility was nil, but the boat plodded along on course, for Mohr had chosen this point south to Charleston as his hunting ground for the night.

"Light on the starboard bow, Herr Kaleu," the lookout reported.

Mohr studied it for a moment. "Frying Pan Buoy,"

he confirmed, then added, "You'd think they'd know Germans can use it as well as Americans."

"Do you suppose they don't know about the war?" Köster asked innocently.

"I'll put you ashore in Charleston and you can tell them," Mohr told him, grinning. "Anyway, I think it's nice of them to leave their navigation lights on for tourists."

"Shadow in sight," Klein cut in, "330 degrees."

Mohr turned to search out the barely visible form.

"Hard port!" he called, not taking his eyes off the ship some 5,000 meters away. "And full speed!"

As Mohr put his boat on a northwesterly course to intercept, he could see that the tanker was not only loaded, but fast.

She was the SS ESSO NASHVILLE, bound for New Haven, Connecticut, with a cargo of 78,000 barrels of black fuel oil from Port Arthur, Texas.

It took nearly an hour running full speed for the U-boat to reach a position to fire a double shot. The first torpedo was a dud, hitting the bow about five feet from the stem on the starboard side, but it did not explode.

The second torpedo hit amidships, exploding with a thundering shock that broke the ship's back.

Reacting instantly, the watch officer on the tanker sounded the general alarm and rang up full speed astern on the engine room telegraph. The radio operator tried to signal a distress call, but the radio shack was filled with suffocating fumes, and he was forced to leave.

All her crew's efforts were futile, and the ship broke in two, the fore part sinking at once. Fifteen minutes after the attack, the ship was abandoned, and attacker and survivors alike left the scene, all assuming the ship was as good as sunk.

Such was not the case, however. Although the fore part of the ship did, indeed, sink, the stern remained afloat and was towed in next day, to be eventually used in the building of a new ship.

Soon after leaving the ESSO NASHVILLE, U-124 made contact with another northbound tanker. She was the MS ATLANTIC SUN, a 11,355 gross ton vessel, en route from Beaumont, Texas, to Marcus Hook, Pennsylvania, with a cargo of crude oil.

Mohr took up the chase, trying in vain to get close enough to attack. But the big tanker was making 16 knots, and Mohr was finding it impossible to get around ahead of her.

"L.I.!" he yelled down the open hatch.

"L.I. here," Subklew answered, below him.

"Twice full speed, Subklew—rev up those diesels! I want that ship!"

"Will do, Herr Kaleu!" Subklew shouted back at him.

The U-Boat shuddered as she picked up speed, circling to get ahead of the tanker. But after an hour's running, she was still unable to get in position to attack, and Mohr knew the tanker had too much speed for him. He would soon lose her altogether.

"Make ready tubes 3 and 4," he ordered finally. "It'll be daylight soon and we're not going to get any closer."

Firing data was passed back to the mixers: "Speed 16 knots; position 116 degrees; distance . . . 3,500 meters . . ."

"Sir?" a voice came back over the speaking tube.

"You heard it," Mohr snapped. "Distance 3,500 meters!"

The torpedoes were fired and sped on their way while the men on the U-boat waited and counted the seconds, then minutes of running time.

After 3 minutes and 21 seconds, one torpedo hit amidships with a bright explosion, and the ship then turned away. U-124 lost contact with her.

ATLANTIC SUN sent out an SOS, which was picked up and acknowledged by Radio Charleston. Both signals were also picked up by the U-boat, which began a search of the area. Visibility had decreased to less than 1,000 meters, and a few bits of wreckage were the only trace she found of the tanker.

Some two and a half hours later, U-124 listened while Charleston tried in vain to raise the ship. Taking this as a distinct possibility that she had sunk, U-124 now pulled out to the 60-meter line. It was daylight now and time to hide at the bottom of the sea.

ATLANTIC SUN, however, was far from sunk, despite the futile efforts of both Radio Charleston and U-124 to renew contact with her.

Her master, Captain R. L. Montague, had, after his initial signal announcing that he had been torpedoed, quietly taken his ship in and anchored off Beaufort Sea Buoy. Later he moved her to Lookout Bight and was able to make temporary repairs before proceeding on to Marcus Hook, arriving a few days late, but with his ship and crew intact.

Prowling the shallow shipping lanes off Hatteras, U-124 was finding the "Golden West" a U-boat paradise that more than lived up to the claims. Here freighters, and best of all—tankers—moved along regular shipping lanes in such numbers that it was not only possible, but necessary, to exercise discrimination in his choice of targets. If only he could have brought a double supply of torpedoes, Mohr thought!

At times, the anti-submarine traffic seemed almost as plentiful as the merchant, but Mohr and his crew felt arrogantly supperior to them in experience and skill, and carried out attacks with brazen disregard for the patrolling ships and planes.

For the most part, the destroyers were little trouble to evade, and they almost never followed a U-boat that turned away. Mohr had to keep reminding himself that there was always a chance of beginner's luck, and he must be careful not to overplay his hand. Diving was, of course, impossible in waters scarcely deep enough to navigate on the surface, and he must not allow himself to be trapped.

The patrol planes appeared too suddenly to allow time to reach water deep enough to dive, but so far their bombing had been mercifully inaccurate. Mohr hoped to God it did not improve.

U-124 was patrolling between Cape Lookout and Cape Fear on the night of March 23. The sky was clear and a bright moon lighted sky and sea. The moon went down early, but visibility remained good.

"Shadow at 10 degrees!" a lookout reported.

Mohr turned to watch the ship about two sea miles away. He ordered a change of course to set up an attack, and could soon make out that she was a freighter of four to five thousand tons, in ballast. She was on a southwest course, and he estimated her speed at about 12 knots.

After about an hour and a quarter of steady running, the boat had closed a considerable part of the distance between them.

"Shadow zero degrees!" a forward lookout called out.

This ship was dead ahead and closing fast. Mohr turned his boat aside and took a close look at the oncoming ship. She was a tanker, and he broke off the attack on the empty freighter for this more valuable prize.

"Full speed on both diesels! Hard port!" Mohr called.

The U-boat turned sharply to come in for a bow shot. Köster called out the firing data. "Distance 900 meters . . . angle 80 degrees . . . speed 11.5 knots . . ." He waited until the cross hairs lay directly midships. "Torpedo . . . los!"

Exactly 16 minutes after first sighting the tanker, the boat fired a torpedo. It missed.

"Distance 700 meters . . ." Köster's impersonal voice gave the readings from the night sight. "Angle 90 degrees . . . speed 11.5 knots . . . los!"

The second torpedo left the tube one minute after the first. It hit under the after mast and set off a blast flame which enveloped the ship. She buckled in the middle and broke apart while both the fore and after parts of the ship sent fountains of flames 100 meters in the air.

The men on the U-boat's bridge watched silently, the glare from the fire reflecting a bloody glow across their tense faces.

There was no catastrophe at sea to compare with a burning tanker, and no more horrible and inescapable death for a seaman.

By sheer will power, Mohr compelled himself to concentrate on her silhouette in an effort to classify her. The unbearable heat kept the boat from approaching closer.

"Gulfbelle type," he finally said, his tone harsh with contradictory emotions. "About 7,000 tons . . ."

"And loaded," Köster added, trying to keep his voice normal and forcing himself to see the holocaust before them only in terms of fuel the Allies could not use against German forces.

Long minutes passed in silence as the U-boat's bridge watch struggled to keep their thoughts away from the tanker's crew, whose blazing pyre held their gaze like a magnet. But try as they might, all they could think of was sailors like themselves, burning and dying in those flames.

"Just like that first tanker," Köster murmured.

"Yes," Mohr answered, turning away.

She was the SS NAECO.

The freighter that Mohr had passed up for the tanker signaled on the 600-meter band, reporting the burning tanker's position.

The NAECO had taken the boat's last torpedo, and brought her score to 7 ships sunk and 3 damaged in the 9-day operation off Cape Hatteras.

That night Mohr signaled a report to Dönitz that his torpedoes were expended and reported unqualified success for the patrol. He described the heavy traffic, a large part of which was tankers, which passed Cape Hatteras in the morning and evening. During the night ships would go from Hatteras to Cape Fear; there was no night traffic between Cape Fear and Charleston. Ships steered from one buoy to the next without going into any of the bays, and light and radio beacons were in operation as though it were peacetime. Destroyers and Coast Guard cutters patrolled around Hatteras and on the shipping lanes, and planes appeared in the evenings. There were no mines.

He listed the ships he had sunk, adding that they had not actually seen the tanker ATLANTIC SUN sink.

Weeks later, Erich Topp, ace commander of U-552, would report these waters still covered with a film of oil, silent witness to Mohr's deadly raid.

At 12:32 on March 23, Mohr sent the following signal to Dönitz: *"Weidmannsdank für freie Jagd. In der Gewitterneumondnacht / war bei Lookout die*

*Tankerschlacht. | Der arme Roosevelt verlor| Fün-
fzigtausend Tonnen. Mohr."* (Hunter's thanks for a
free hunt. In the stormy new moon night / was by
Lookout the tanker fight. / The poor Roosevelt lost /
fifty thousand tons. Mohr.)

Several hours later, he received the following signal
from Dönitz: *"An Mohr | Gut gemacht. —Befehlsha-
ber."* (Well done.)

The success off Cape Hatteras had boosted Mohr's
tonnage score past the 100,000-ton mark, and the crew
knew the Knight's Cross would be waiting for him
when he got home. So they had, as they had once
done for Schulz, secretly made a Knight's Cross themselves. When the expected announcement came, their
Mohr would wear his new decoration at once, without
having to wait for Dönitz. So the black cross, trimmed
with silver, and hung on a black and white ribbon,
was carefully made by Mechanikermaat Loba and
hidden away.

When the signal arrived announcing Mohr's decoration, the officer on watch quietly tucked it in his
pocket, and everyone on board became engaged in
the conspiracy. There was suddenly much subdued
activity and excitement, and Mohr was the only one
who was unaware of it.

To the everlasting delight of the crew, U-124 sport-
ed a wondrously skilled pastry chef, and he brought
his full talents into play as he baked a magnificent
cake for the commander. It was elaborately decorated
with a Knight's Cross in icing in the center, and
around the edge were the words, *"Der Mohr hat
seiner Schuldigkeit getan,"* quoted from Dönitz's famous signal to Mohr at the end of his first patrol as
commander. Mohr had indeed done his duty!

Hours later, when this masterpiece was ready, it
was carried to the bridge, along with the wireless

signal and the home-made Knight's Cross. An added
festive touch was another signal from Headquarters
which announced that U-124's chief engineering officer
had been promoted to Kapitänleutnant and the II
watch officer to Oberleutnant.

While the elaborate preparations were being carried out, Mohr lay worn out and sound asleep in his
bunk, oblivious to it all.

"Commander to the bridge!"

The loud shout rang through the boat, jarring the
exhausted Mohr back to consciousness. His feet were
on the deck before he was more than half awake.
Ship in sight? Plane attacking? He rounded the corner
at a run, bumping his head and swearing angrily.

He popped up on the bridge sleepy, bewildered,
and bad-tempered, rubbing his head and muttering to
himself. He was greeted with laughter and congratulations from the group on the bridge, and ceremoniously presented with his cake, the wireless message from
Dönitz, and the Knight's Cross, which was fastened
around his neck.

Mohr's bad humor vanished at once and he grinned
in boyish delight at the surprises. The black and silver
medal shone brightly against his grimy undershirt,
and from that day he would wear it all the time,
whether he had on a fresh white dress shirt or none at
all. When they arrived at base, he would receive the
decoration and congratulations from Dönitz, but the
Knight's Cross he always wore was the one his men
had made.

Chapter Eleven

U-124, AFTER only a short overhauling, put to sea on May 4, 1942. Her last cruise had been a lone wolf operation, but this time she was part of a pack, identified by the code name Gruppe Hecht. The other commanders in the pack were Ites, Hinsch, Dieterichs, Müller-Edzards, Rehwinkel, and Bülow.

Dönitz believed the British would be using the shipping lanes along the Great Circle again since his blitzkrieg on the U.S. coast had left the convoys for a time relatively unmolested. If his guess were right, and the British had indeed gone back to this shortest sea route, then a well-placed wolf pack could reap a big harvest.

He was right. Even before the boats could take up their positions, U-124 intercepted a signal from Hinsch in U-569 to the BdU reporting contact with the westbound Convoy ONS 92. An hour later Mohr was able to report, *"Habe Fühling"* (have contact). Dönitz signaled the other boats to close in, and released Mohr and Hinsch to attack as soon as another boat sighted the convoy.

Ites reported contact, and by 0115 on May 12,

U-124 had reached a shooting position. The convoy was ranged in three columns, and the U-boat had come in between the left and middle columns on a reciprocal course. Mohr fired a double shot at a loaded freighter, and both torpedoes hit. The 6,000-ton ship stopped, her bow settling so deeply into the water that her screws were out.

Another smaller freighter, also loaded and deep in the water, was the target for a stern shot.

". . . 90 degrees . . . distance, 1500 meters . . ." The torpedo officer waited until the ship came into the sight. "Los!"

The torpedo hit just abaft the smoke stack, and with the detonation came bedlam.

The freighter fired a signal flare amid the banshee howl of sirens as she began sinking by the stern. Within 10 minutes she was under, and U-124 was out of the convoy.

Other ships in the convoy were now shooting flares in a frantic attempt to either expose the U-boat or frighten her away.

Mohr's grey eyes flickered in the light from the star shells as he watched the convoy lying dispersed along the whole northern horizon in front of him. About 20 ships were silhouetted by the brilliant flares they had fired for protection.

"Look at that," Mohr said. "There they are—like on a serving tray!"

U-124, safe and undetected on the dark south horizon, now came around on a new course to take her back into the convoy. He quickly fired two bow shots on two overlapping freighters. The first torpedo hit its target amidships and the ship broke open. She sank in three minutes. The second torpedo missed.

As the U-boat turned off toward the darkened south horizon, the sharp silhouette of a corvette suddenly appeared directly ahead, no more than 200 meters away. She was traveling at high speed, and she had blocked Mohr's way into the dark.

"Hard starboard!" he yelled. "Full speed!"

U-124 heeled over away from the escort and back into the freighter column. Her own diesels roaring as she pounded through the heavy seas, she passed between two freighters whose sirens were howling with a maddening shriek.

"Escort on the starboard bow!" a lookout screamed above the fury.

No sooner had Mohr turned the boat away from this threat than another lookout reported a corvette to port.

Watching both escorts, Mohr held his boat in the middle and went between them. For an anxious moment, the U-boat lay with an escort abeam both starboard and port, each only 800 meters away. Then she was past them, plunging into the middle column of ships.

Mohr fired a stern shot with the last torpedo left in the tubes. It hit a 3,000-ton freighter amidships. Then he pulled out to reload.

Anxious not to lose the convoy, Mohr took time to load only three tubes before starting back. Another dazzling burst of star shells hung over the convoy, and Mohr wondered if they were for another U-boat.

Back in the middle column of the convoy, Mohr shot one torpedo at a 3,000-ton freighter. Hit amidships, she stopped, and within six minutes, her whole stern was under water. Mohr fired his other bow torpedo at another ship, but missed.

Wheeling around, he fired a stern shot at a ship behind him. This one hit just forward of the bridge. Shooting star shells frantically, the ship began settling by the stern. Mohr watched as the water rose till the forward hatches were covered. Seven minutes after the torpedo struck, the ship was gone.

As Mohr turned his boat toward the covering darkness, he could see red flashes from two of the ships in the middle of the convoy.

"Muzzle fire," he said to the I.WO. "Looks like a 2 cm. machine gun, and they're shooting down. Wonder who's the target?"

Then across the water came the sound of detonations unmistakable to a U-boat man—depth charges.

The I.WO looked at the commander. "Hinsch or Ites—or maybe they're just to scare us off." The latter was the preferred assumption. It was not pleasant to imagine a brother U-boat the target of those hellish Wabos.

Dawn had lighted the eastern sky as U-124 pulled out. Mohr sent the convoy position and his additional sinkings in to headquarters, then lost contact. There had been no report from either Hinsch or Ites since 0430.

A few hours later Mohr caught sight of a single freighter, and quickly reported that he had regained contact with the convoy. Shortly afterward, Hinsch and Ites both reported that they were in contact. Dieterich's boat had also found it. Now Gruppe Hecht had placed four boats against the convoy.

Near noon, one of the lookouts reported a German boat in sight. As they closed, they recognized Dieterich's boat, and waved a greeting.

The radio man handed Mohr a signal he had picked up. Hellriegel had reported contact. Now there were five.

"Escort ship . . ." a lookout reported.

The "Stork" type escort was close, and as Mohr turned his boat away he suddenly found himself on the verge of ramming Dieterichs.

"Hard port!" he yelled.

The boat swung out of the way of the approaching U-boat, and Mohr caught sight of U-Hellriegel. The three boats were coming in together on the port side of the convoy.

Another signal came in, this time from Müller-Edzards, reporting contact. And now there were six.

Weather conditions had deteriorated and the attacking wolf pack found itself in constant rain through the day and night.

An escort fired several salvoes, apparently at Dieterichs, then turned away as Dieterichs turned toward U-124.

Another destroyer suddenly loomed up out of the rain on the port quarter, but she was soon lost to sight as U-124 held her course.

As the rain reduced visibility to practically nothing, the fast-ranging destroyers kept the boats away from the merchant ships until the whole pack had lost contact.

In an effort to renew the attack, Dönitz directed the Gruppe Hecht boats into a reconaissance line, but it was the next day before Hellriegel reported sighting a single destroyer. The rest of the pack spent the next day and night trying vainly to intercept, and on May 15, Dieterichs reported contact, but with another convoy.

Five days passed as the wolf pack searched fruitlessly for convoys.

On May 20, Dieterichs sighted the westbound Convoy ONS 94, but he was forced under by a destroyer. He gave his last position report, adding the depressing information that the convoy was going into a fog bank.

Hellriegel also reported fog, and the pack was unable to attack. Dönitz again strung his U-boats in a line south of Newfoundland.

Mohr, blinded by fog, repeatedly dived to listen for the sound of screws, and twice was able to hear them. But both times the distant sounds were gone before he had a chance to pursue.

In the meantime, the big mine-laying boat, U-116 (von Schmidt), which had been fitted out as a U-tanker, had arrived in the area about 600 miles south of Cape Race to supply the boats of Gruppe Hecht. U-124 was ordered to rendezvous with her on May 25.

The provisioning took several days, and the bone-tired U-124 crew rested and relaxed. Optimistic fishermen rigged their lines in ambitious but futile hopes of catching a whale, or at least a sea turtle. They were duly photographed by Matrosen Wenig, who along with the meteorologist Dr. Walden, was a guest on board U-124 for the cruise.

U-96 also joined the rendezvous, and her commander, Oblt. z. S. Hellriegel, came aboard U-124 for a visit.

U-124 took on 12 torpedoes, 132 cbm. diesel oil, and provisions for seven weeks, then left the "Milch cow" to return to the hunt.

During the latter part of May, all the boats were refueled, and by June 1, had been formed into another line across the Great Circle.

They were in almost constant touch with each other and with headquarters, exchanging news of all sorts, relevant or not. Birthday greetings, jokes, and personal comments by the commanders to each other spiced otherwise routine signals or were sent out alone. This went on until Dönitz, apparently annoyed by the trivia they were announcing to him, each other, and anyone else who happened to be tuned in, finally signaled the boats of Gruppe Hecht to shut up unless they had something to report.

The Naval Cryptographic Service informed Dönitz that they had decoded British signals indicating that a new convoy, ONS 100, was due to sail. Accordingly, the admiral regrouped his wolf pack, and on June 6, the first boat made contact.

Müller-Edzards reported sighting the convoy, but a few minutes later he added a second report, saying that he had been forced under and had lost contact.

Dönitz signaled, releasing Müller-Edzards for a daylight attack. He repeatedly regained contact with the convoy, only to lose it, and although he sent a directional signal to Mohr, neither boat was able to attack.

And again Dönitz called off the group to form a reconnaissance line, this time in mid-Atlantic.

On June 8, Mohr sighted a convoy, and the pack began to close in. Hinsch made contact the next day, but Mohr was still unable to get past the escorts to the convoy.

He fired two stern shots at the destroyer on the starboard side, but both missed, and U-124 was still blocked out by the escorts.

Mohr fell back to try to slip in past the after escort, but the destroyer was zig-zagging too fast to give the U-boat a chance. Visibility was too good.

Frustrated and exasperated, Mohr turned his sights on the offending escort, firing a salvo of two torpedoes. A hit close to the after stack sent a broad geyser of water flying into the air and shock waves of sound rumbling across the water. A second explosion, undoubtedly from her boilers, enveloped the destroyer in clouds of steam.

Rolling thunder from exploding depth charges and

small enough to be carried on escort vessels and aircraft. And when enough escorts were equipped with it, this device would spell the end of the free-for-all wolf pack attacks with which the U-boats had slaughtered the hard-pressed convoys. With radar, the darkest night would not hide a surfaced U-boat, and the destroyers would hunt them down as relentlessly as the U-boats had dogged the convoys.

Still uneasy, in spite of Mohr's opinion, the BdU decided to break off the operation on June 18. U-124 turned her bow eastward and set her course for Lorient. Her success was high—seven ships sunk and two others hit, but it had been a grueling cruise.

The off-watch crew had turned in, glad to be head-ed home. Mohr was asleep in his bunk, utterly exhausted after some five weeks of convoy battles. For the first time since the first convoy was spotted, he could now look forward to uninterrupted sleep and he had fallen into his bunk in blissful anticipation. He had been asleep less than an hour.

"Commander to the bridge! !"

Now what? Mohr grabbed his jacket and started for the bridge, his body automatically obeying the summons even before his mind was fully awake.

"What is it?"

"Convoy, Herr Kaleu. There, off the port bow."

Mohr's own battle report records the action:

"18.6 0230. Wireless sent. Setting out on return. . . . 0600. Daybreak, shadow in sight off port bow toward the east. . . . convoy . . . hard evasive maneuver because of destroyer. Passed at about 300 meters, didn't see us. . . . running with high speed northward so as to place me on the starboard side. Convoy goes northwest. 1618. Becoming brighter, can look the situation over. Convoy steams in 2 columns, right column has 5 big ships, left at least 3 large ships, columns tightly covered by small craft. One destroyer is forward side escort. Boat stands on the inside of the forward escort, exactly in front of the left column. Around 0620 I turn around for a bow shot attack on the leading ship of the right column. Shoot a two-torpedo spread on the right ship, a freighter of 7,000 tons, position 40 degrees, distance 4,000 meters. Immediately a two-torpedo spread at the second and third ships which follow close together, each freighter 6,000 tons. Distance 4,000 meters. Two hits on the lead ship after 4 minutes 16 seconds running time. Black smoke cloud from the explosion, over 100 meters high. Ship sinks quickly. After 3 minutes part of the ship towers up out of the water, after 5 minutes, it is gone. At the same time a hit on second ship of 6,000 tons, bright blaze of fire, rain of sparks. Freighter falls away aft, apparently has internal fires. After 6 minutes fires are extinguished as freighter sinks. A minute later torpedo detonation heard in boat. Hit not observed on surface. Hit on third ship, freighter of 6,000 tons is assumed. After the shots on the surface, I go full speed northward to break through ahead of the starboard escort. No flares, it is quite light . . ."

The boat was soon well away from the convoy, and Mohr once again turned toward Lorient.

"How do we stand on fuel?" he asked Subklew.

"We've got enough," Subklew told him. "But just barely, at the most economical cruising speed."

"Well, take your time," Mohr told him. "We're not running a race."

While U-124 cruised home, Laubisch made the pennants to fly when she entered port.

As soon as his official duties in port were finished,

Mohr headed for Berlin and his wife. He had a long leave coming, and it was a particularly enjoyable one.

His wife was expecting a child, and the imminent prospect of fatherhood filled him with awe and pride. Eva insisted that it must be a son, but her husband confided, to her surprise, that he would really much rather have a daughter first. Preferably, just like her mother.

But frequent air raids on Berlin sounded an ominous note, and with growing concern for his wife's safety, Mohr began quietly to make plans to send her to a safer place.

Mohr's brother, Theo, was also on leave and visited them in Berlin. He was a sergeant pilot in the Luftwaffe, and it was a rare and precious time for the two brothers to spend a leave together. They took long walks, relishing the beauty of Berlin in summer, and talked far into the night.

By way of variety, one day Jochen insisted that they exchange uniforms before their walk. So he wore Theo's sergeant's uniform, while Theo was attired as a naval officer, complete with Knight's Cross.

They met an army captain on the street who turned to stare perplexedly at them after they passed. For he had received a dazzling salute from a navy lieutenant wearing the U-boat pin and Knight's Cross, while the Luftwaffe sergeant accompanying him had made a lackadaisical wave of his arm that was more of a gesture than a salute. The captain shook his head and walked on. War nerves, no doubt.

"Jochen!" hissed Theo at his side. "You've got to salute better than that! Somebody will stop us and then we'll both be in the soup!"

"All right," laughed Jochen, and promised to greet all future officers in a manner more befitting a sergeant.

They were like little boys, laughing and carefree. Full of jokes and pranks, they lived these golden days to the fullest, almost as though they knew it was the last such leisurely time they would ever spend together.

Even with trips back and forth to Lorient to check on the boat and talk to the flotilla commander, Mohr was able to spend much time at home during the summer and fall.

A cousin whose husband had just been killed came to stay with them for a few weeks in the fall. The young widow seemed so calm and self-controlled that Eva remarked to Jochen about how strange it seemed. He nodded seriously and replied, "She does the right thing. You must not show others your grief. Always keep those things to yourself. That's the best way."

Perhaps he intended the words for Eva herself. For in the black days to come, she would remember them. She would also remember and draw comfort from Admiral Dönitz's words to her, "Remember what I tell you; your husband is the best horse in my stable."

The boat had been given an extensive overhauling, and then, when it was almost time to sail again, an unexpected event delayed her for several more weeks. There was an Allied air raid on the base at Lorient, which caught U-124 being moved from one bunker to another. As long as the boats were in the reinforced concrete U-boat pens, air raids could not hurt them, but to be caught outside was another matter.

Two bombs fell close to U-124, wounding two men. There was no visible damage to the boat, but the sailing date had to be postponed a month so she could be thoroughly checked again.

It was to this air raid that Mohr owed his presence at home for the birth of his son, who was given the same name as the father, Johann Hendrick Mohr. When asked if he were not disappointed that it was not a girl, he laughed and confessed that his big show of wanting a daughter instead of a son was only an act calculated at soothing his wife's disappointment in case their baby had been a girl.

And now that he was the father of a son, Mohr quit smoking cigarettes. A man of such dignity and stature was better suited to cigars, he declared ceremoniously.

Next day he headed back to Lorient.

Chapter Twelve

THE FREE-wheeling U-boats had, since the first of the year, turned the Western Atlantic into a shambles.

The first ten days of the Paukenschlag attack had netted 25 ships with about 200,000 gross register tons. And that was only the beginning.

In January, 35 ships were sunk in American waters, and in February, 45. In March, losses climbed to 76 ships, and dropped back to 52 in April.

Then in May, U-boats sank 105 ships in the western Atlantic. They found the Gulf of Mexico to be indeed the "Promised Land," and in May alone sank 41 ships of 219,867 tons in this one area. It was the most ships to be sunk in one area in any one month of the entire war.

June saw sinkings in American waters climb to the frightful total of 110 ships. So in the first half of 1942, U-boats had claimed 472 merchant ships in the western Atlantic. To make it worse, a large percentage of these losses were tankers.

The rampage continued unchecked through the year. As American defenses tightened up along the Atlantic seaboard, Dönitz moved his boats into the

Gulf. When escorted convoys were formed there, he pulled them out into the Caribbean. And so it went. As soon as the defenses stiffened in one area, the U-boats left it to strike unexpectedly in some unprotected spot.

There were thousands of miles of brightly lit coastline to protect, and the harrassed American U-boat hunters could not be everywhere at once. Short on numbers, experience, and organization, they could not begin to cope with the onslaught.

The day would come when American hunter-killer groups with carrier-based aircraft would seek and destroy U-boats all over the Atlantic. But in 1942, when U-boats were sinking ships by the score in sight of American cities, that day seemed a long way off.

When still only a few days out from Lorient on this, her tenth war cruise, Mohr received a signal from the BdU telling him that a quantity of diesel oil in Lorient had been sabotaged, and it was from this supply that U-124 had filled her bunkers. A chemical added to the oil would cause the fuel pumps to corrode, jamming the fuel injector valves, and Dönitz requested a report on the condition of U-124's engines.

Mohr replied that he was having trouble with the injector valves, and that at least one fuel pump was already corroded.

Dönitz signaled Mohr, Nissen, and Rüggeberg, all of whose boats had taken on sabotaged oil, to run for a whole day at full speed. They were then to decide whether to go on or return to base.

After this trial run, Mohr reported the port diesel clear but he had to replace a fuel pump and two valves in the starboard diesel. He added that he could still operate, and requested that he be given an extra fuel pump when he refueled.

Next day he met the U-tanker U-118 and took on 300 liters of lubricating oil and 20 cbm. diesel oil. Since this fuel was good, it was held in reserve for attacks while the boat continued to cruise on the bad oil. U-124 also got a small quantity of food stuff, one reserve fuel pump, two valves, and 150 potassium cartridges.

By the time the boat reached her operational area in the western Atlantic, one diesel or the other was being repaired nearly every day.

On the evening of December 15, while still 700 sea miles east of Trinidad, U-124 made contact with a westbound convoy reported by U-Emmermann four days earlier.

It was past midnight when Mohr got a chance to slip into the convoy. He fired a double shot at the starboard escort which zig-zagged into firing position, but the fast ship turned and the torpedoes missed.

But U-124 was now into the convoy. Mohr could make out six ships, high in ballast, and four of them were tankers. Five destroyers guarded them.

Mohr torpedoed two of the tankers, two minutes apart. The first sank in 15 minutes; the second broke apart and sank in 5 minutes.

Crossing out of the convoy, U-124 reloaded her torpedo tubes. As she started back to the convoy, she was forced under by a plane and was unable to regain contact.

Still traveling west, the boat sighted another small convoy of tankers. Mohr ordered her hard port and full speed ahead.

No sooner had the boat swung into the turn and her screws bit deeper into the water as the engines shuddered into the increased revs than she faltered, then slowed again.

"Commander to L.I.!" Mohr called down the hatch.

Subklew's face appeared below him. "L.I. here!"

"What's the matter?"

"Starboard diesel is out, Herr Kaleu. Dead. *Kaputt.*"

"Oh hell," growled Mohr, watching the tankers disappear. "Break off the attack. Secure from battle stations."

Subklew and his men worked through the night on the diesels, and by morning had them in running order again. The boat resumed her course west while her commander and L.I. speculated on how long the repairs would hold up this time.

"Commander to the bridge!"

Mohr and Subklew were in the wardroom drinking coffee when the call blared over the loudspeaker.

A minute later Mohr was on the bridge studying the faint line on the horizon that was a ship. It took the rest of the afternoon to bring the boat around to a position ahead of the freighter, and at last in the gathering dusk, Mohr submerged to wait for the ship to cross his bow.

But while he was making his final calculations, the ship set her running lights and lit up her neutral markings.

"Secure from attack," Mohr said. "She's neutral."

U-124 surfaced, and the men on the bridge watched until the ship was out of sight.

Engine trouble had become more than a nuisance on this cruise. Diesels that stopped without warning and refused to run for hours not only cost the boat success in the form of sunk ships, but put her in grave danger as well. Consolidated bombers flew over with alarming frequency, and only a sound and alert boat could hope to get safely under before the bombs fell. Mohr noted with regret that their aim had improved dangerously.

In spite of the difficulties besetting her, however,

U-124 continued to sink ships. And as usual, she celebrated Christmas at sea, receiving holiday greetings from the BdU along with U-Achilles, which was close by.

A few days after Christmas, while the boat was a few miles off the Tobago coast, Mohr decided to move in close to Trinidad. About dark, Subklew filled up the batteries with distilled water to have them in readiness. But there was salt in the distilled water, and within minutes, the batteries began to give off the deadly chlorine gas.

Mohr brought her to the surface, and it took the next twelve hours or so to ventilate the boat.

"What next?" murmured Mohr, clearly disappointed and thoroughly frustrated. Engine trouble had dogged his heels since they left the Bay of Biscay, and had spoiled attack after attack.

Subklew shrugged and shook his head. "I'd like to get my hands on whoever ruined that oil. I've sure earned my pay this cruise!"

Mohr looked at him and smiled. It was true. The poor L.I. had already done more repair work on the diesels than an engineer might ordinarily expect to do in several cruises.

"What do you think?" Mohr asked him quietly. "Will they hold up for the rest of the patrol?"

"I don't know," Subklew answered. "If we just had all good fuel and could throw this crap away—but we have to keep burning it, and it keeps tearing the engines up as fast as we can get them fixed." He paused. "But I do know this, Herr Kaleu'nt. You've got to be very careful with the engines. I'll do the best I can for you in an attack. But when I have to stop them, I just have to stop them. You can't push the diesels this trip or they're going to fly to pieces and we can swim home."

"OK, L.I.," Mohr told him, "you're boss in the engine room."

Perhaps Mohr remembered Brinker's words, "You must listen to your L.I." He did not have Schulz's understanding of engineering, but Brinker had finally succeeded in teaching him that diesels, unlike men, had their limits, and trying to push them beyond these limits would only get him in trouble. And Mohr had learned to rely on Subklew as he had on Brinker. It did not really matter to him if the boat ran on diesel oil or witchcraft as long as he had an L.I. who could handle her.

The state of the engines by now might well have given another commander a first-class case of the jitters. But Mohr had held onto his nerves and his sense of humor, and if he ever felt jumpy or irritable, he managed to keep it hidden from his officers and men.

And largely through his efforts and example, he prevented the feelings of frustration and futility that might have drained the aggressive spirit from his crew. Close as they were to land—often within sight— he nevertheless allowed them to spend as much time as possible on the upper deck while repairs were going on. This gave them at least a temporary escape from the suffocating heat inside the boat. And with the diesels out of whack they would be helpless in the face of an attack anyway, so it did not matter whether the crew was standing at battle stations or lying on the upper deck asleep in the sun. Being sighted would mean being sunk.

In a gesture of outrageous impudence, Mohr had a toilet seat attached to the rail so that it was suspended over the side, thus giving U-124 the distinction of being the only ship at sea with an outdoor john. With this unique arrangement, the crew could show exactly how much awe and terror they felt for "Britain's Ocean" while enjoying fresh air and sunshine unknown in the confines of Tube 7.

On the night of December 28, U-124 sighted a 4,000-ton freighter as she came in close to Trinidad. The calm sea and bright moonlight made a U-boat on the surface entirely too conspicuous, so Mohr made a submerged attack with a stern shot. The torpedo hit, and in less than one minute the stem of the freighter was under water.

When the ship sank, Mohr brought his boat to the surface. It would soon be daylight, and he wanted to get well away from this shallow water with its scattered wreckage. He saw a survivor on a raft nearby, so he turned toward him to try to find out the name of the ship and her cargo. But as soon as the boat approached the man, he dived off the raft in fright.

Frowning, Mohr turned the boat away.

With daylight, U-124 moved northward, circling around Tobago and into the Caribbean. Soon after dark that evening, she spotted two tankers and took up the chase. They were close together, and the boat followed them close inshore to Trinidad. Mohr fired four torpedoes, two for each ship.

The ships steamed serenely on their way as all four torpedoes proved faulty and came nowhere near their intended victims, but instead wound up on the beach with a roar that alerted all Trinidad.

A short time later, in response to these outlaw torpedoes, a Catalina appeared, flying low. It had no trouble finding the offending U-boat on this bright clear night, her wake gleaming in the smooth water.

The plane flew directly over the boat, then circled to come back again. The bridge watch looked at Mohr. It was high time to dive. The plane had found them and taken their measure, and now was coming back to drop bombs.

Mohr shook his head in answer to their unspoken question. "We stay on the surface," he said. "I want those tankers, and they're long gone if we have to hit the cellar."

The plane flew over the boat again. Still no bombs. But again it turned to come back.

"They may not have any bombs," Mohr said. Then he added quietly, "But don't take any bets on it."

He held the boat steady on her course while this nerve-wracking inspection was going on. The third time the plane flew over, it was even lower and the bomb bay doors were open. Mohr stood motionless, his grey eyes hard as steel, his gaze never wavering from the plane which had now turned to make a fourth pass over the U-boat.

This was a different Mohr from the boyish skipper joking in the wardroom or rigging a toilet seat to perch precariously over the ocean. This was all U-boat commander, all fighter, bold, hard, and brilliant. He knew precisely what he was doing, the risk he was taking, and his chances of bringing it off. And while the plane was flying back and forth across the U-boat, getting ready to attack, Mohr was also sizing up his opponent. It had taken iron nerves to hold the boat steady on her course during the plane's feints, but when the moment came, he would be ready.

The Catalina came in for the fourth run. It was low and steady on course, headed straight for them.

Mohr watched, gauging the distance. Now!

"Hard starboard!"

The boat heeled over, answering the helm instantly. Seconds later, two bombs fell from the plane, spiraling directly for the boat.

But Mohr had guessed the moment precisely, and

the bombs fell, one on each side of the boat, no more than four or five meters away. The turn had saved her.

"Alarm!" Mohr shouted. "Dive, Subklew! 2A plus 60! Alarm!"

The bridge watch fled pell-mell down the hatch with Mohr on top of them. He had already scrambled down the ladder to the control room before the shout to Subklew was out of his mouth.

Subklew drove the boat under at top speed. "Everybody forward!" he yelled above the confusion, and wildly running men skidded into and over each other as they added their own weight to that of the sea water rushing into the diving tanks.

The bombs had been too close and now the boat, damaged to an unknown degree, threatened to go out of control in her headlong dive.

Officers and men in the control room fought frantically to handle her as wheels spun uselessly under shattered dials.

"Here, grab this!" Subklew yelled at the commander, turning over the diving planes controls to him while he and the petty officers managed finally to bring the boat under control.

Leveling off at last, Subklew and his men made repairs to the damaged equipment while Mohr operated the diving planes.

The boat continued on a northerly course, surfacing some seven hours later.

A few days later, Mohr spotted a convoy just north of British Guiana, but soon after he started chasing it, both diesels stopped, leaving the boat dead in the water all afternoon while repairs were made to the pumps and valves.

The boat was dangerously close to the enemy coast, and helpless without the engines, but again their luck held. The men whiled away the afternoon fishing for the sharks that circled the boat.

The champion fisherman proved to be Oberleutnant zur See Willi Gerlach. A former merchant sailor, Gerlach could have been lifted straight from a Jack London story. He was so animated and vigorous, so surrounded by an aura of adventure and excitement, that it was easy to imagine him as captain of a windjammer, plying the South Sea islands. Now he stood on the U-boat's deck, skillfully hauling the big sharks alongside, then killing them with pistol shots. Shark meat provided a change in the menu, but the fierce odor while it was cooking detracted more than a little from the fairly good taste.

U-124 continued her patrol from Trinidad west along the northern coast of South America, frequently in sight of land. She sank ships traveling singly and in convoy, often having the use of only one or the other diesel for an attack.

The area was under constant surveillance by the Consolidated bombers, but they miraculously failed to appear when both diesels failed.

On January 9, U-124 made contact with the first of the Trinidad-Bahia convoys, Convoy TB 1, east of Trinidad. A lookout on the bridge sighted a star shell fired over the horizon just after midnight.

One diesel was out of order, but repairs were finished while the boat headed toward the flare on one engine. Three hours later, the boat had the convoy in sight and she moved along with the merchantmen in a southeasterly direction, easily holding contact as the escorts appeared to be inexperienced. There were nine loaded ships in the convoy, and Mohr could count four destroyers.

It was nearly dawn when the boat submerged to attack. Mohr fired a three-torpedo spread at two overlapping freighters. Two of the torpedoes missed the lead freighter to hit an 8,000-ton tanker ahead of her.

A gasoline explosion sent a white blast flame soaring 400 meters high—then the whole ship was afire with leaping yellow oil flames. The blazing tanker lay with her bow deep in the water, lighting the whole scene with garish brilliance and hung a pall of black smoke over the sky.

The third torpedo hit the first freighter with a loud explosion. Small bright lights flickered from lifeboats that moved away as she broke apart and sank.

Crossing through the convoy, Mohr reloaded the bow tubes, then came in for another bow shot at two more freighters. Both hit, and both ships sank within five minutes.

He fired a double stern shot at two other overlapping freighters, but both torpedoes hit the same ship. She broke apart amidships and sank.

U-124 turned away from an approaching destroyer and into a rain squall. All her torpedo tubes were empty, but Mohr was desperately trying to hold contact with the convoy. She was steering into shallow water, and the approaching dawn would soon make it too dangerous for him to remain close. He could not afford to let daylight catch him in waters too shallow to dive.

The tanker was still burning like a torch, and star shells and searchlights added their own white and yellow brilliance to the blood red glow from the flames leaping into the air.

The glaring light played across the faces of the men on the U-boat's bridge as they watched the floundering remnants of the convoy. Daylight and shallow water under their keels would give the merchantmen a measure of safety in which to salvage what ships and lives they could until darkness came again.

U-124, her fangs drawn, could only try to hold contact until she had a chance to attack again.

Mohr signaled his success to Dönitz: he had sunk the tanker SS BROAD ARROW, of nearly 8,000 tons, the 6,194-ton SS BIRMINGHAM CITY, the 5,101-ton COLLINGSWORTH, the 4,553-ton SS MINOTAUR, all American ships, and one other freighter.

By the time his signal had gone out, both diesels stopped, and repairs took another 12 hours to complete. The convoy was gone.

Next day one diesel went out during a chase after a single ship. Mohr tried to operate on one engine, then at high speed on both electric motors. He finally got into position to fire a salvo, only to miss the target.

One diesel was clear, but now the gyrocompass was not working. The freighter, which had apparently seen the torpedoes that missed, started zig-zagging.

Mohr had managed to get his crippled boat back into position with one diesel and the magnetic compass when Subklew informed him that both diesels were now clear. Mohr answered by ordering twice full speed on both.

The radio room reported a signal from the freighter: "W F C Y. Attack by German submarine—immediately afterward 3 torpedoes — S-S-S — I am chased — S-S-S."

A Consolidated plane answered the ship's call for help and forced U-124 under before she could attack again.

Throughout the next few days, Consolidateds kept watch over the area, preventing any further chance of attack.

On January 16, Mohr fired one torpedo at a tanker. It missed, and when he got in closer, he could see her neutral flag, and broke off the attack. Two days later, he got in position to attack another tanker at dusk, but broke off when she set her running lights.

With both diesels alternately breaking down and being repaired, U-124 finally rendezvoused with a U-tanker to refuel for the trip home. She had sunk three tankers and five freighters for an estimated total of 46,000 tons.

She arrived back at Lorient on February 13, 1943, her cruise highly successful despite the constant engine trouble.

Both Gerlach and Subklew left the boat for good after this patrol. Subklew was transferred to Pilau, a training base on the Baltic in East Prussia, and Gerlach would soon receive a command of his own.

While still at sea, Mohr had been notified that he was awarded the Oak Leaves to the Knight's Cross, the 177th man in the German Armed Forces to receive this decoration.

But this time, instead of receiving his medal from his own men on the bridge of his own boat, Mohr was flown in state to the Ukraine to have it presented by the Führer himself. He later described the four-hour meeting with Hitler non-committally as "very interesting."

Having been brought up in a family atmosphere of dislike for the Nazi party, he shared his father's feelings. But with Germany at war and fighting for her life, he, like many others, felt that Nazis or no, they were all in the same boat. The political situation could be straightened out after the war, but for the moment, Germany and her survival came first—a view that was naive and perhaps over-optimistic, but by no means uncommon.

Mohr spent a brief leave with his wife and young son, and for the first time, Eva managed to conceal her fear and heartbreak when he left. She was laughing and gay as she saw him off, and Jochen was out of sight before her tears came. But she knew this was to be his last cruise and then he would be transferred to shore and safe.

He would write her a letter when he reached the boat, to be posted just before he sailed, and tell her how proud he was of his "brave wife," and how much easier it was for him because she had told him good-bye with a smile.

En route to Lorient, he stopped off for a short visit with his brother. Theo was soon to leave for the Russian front. He would be reported as missing in action, and his family would wait for further word for years. But nothing else would be heard, and he would never return.

Mohr then went on to Nantes, where he stopped overnight, waiting for train connections on to Lorient. As he walked across the railway station, he suddenly came face to face with a young sailor trudging along, sea bag slung over his shoulder. It was Karl Kesselheim.

Since they were both waiting for the same train next morning, they decided to celebrate the unexpected reunion properly. They got a room at a nearby hotel and cleaned up for dinner. Kesselheim was wearing sea boots, and since his shoes were at the very bottom of his sea bag, Mohr loaned him a pair of his own, which fit quite well. When Kesselheim could not find his own razor, he shaved with Mohr's.

When they had made themselves presentable, Mohr led the way to the Officers' Club for dinner. On the way, they discussed the matter at length and decided the one thing they most wanted was chicken. But when they got there, they found the club full of

Italian officers—and nothing but spaghetti on the menu.

After dinner, they found a night club nearby and bribed the waiter to give them the only vacant table left, which had been reserved. They settled themselves comfortably, near a group of high-ranking officers and their dates, and unconcernedly rode out the storm of protest when a party of indignant officers appeared looking for their usurped reservation.

The atmosphere in the club was as gay as tinsel, and they drank and talked about all that had happened to them since Kesselheim left the boat. All the original crew of the U-124 was gone by now, Mohr told him. Many of them had left when Schulz did, and his only request to Mohr when he gave the boat over to him was that he get all the old crew posted to shore stations as soon as he could.

Promptly at midnight, one of the officers at the nearby table rose and came over to them. He introduced himself as the post commander of Nantes, and told Mohr that since his companion was a petty officer, he would have to leave. Only officers were exempt from the midnight curfew, and petty officers had to be home by twelve.

Mohr informed him placidly that they were both in transit and in no way connected with the Nantes garrison. Therefore the curfew did not apply to them.

The post commander left, but soon returned with reinforcements in the form of another officer. With a wary glance at Mohr's decorations, he told him that it did not matter who he was or where he was going, while in Nantes, he would have to bow to local regulation. He could stay, but his companion would have to leave.

At this, Mohr flushed scarlet with anger. "The petty

officer and I are friends and we are together," he informed them hotly. "There are two of us and that makes four fists. And if you have anything else to say, we can settle it outside!"

The two officers withdrew, shocked and horrified. And the subject of Kesselheim's leaving was closed for good.

Kesselheim had sat silent through Mohr's startling outburst, content to let him talk their way out of it, or perfectly willing to join him in a fist fight with two high-ranking officers if Mohr wished.

Now they sat back to enjoy their wine, the incident finished and soon forgotten. Their adversaries apparently forgot it too, and a short time later invited them over to their table for a drink. By the time the night club closed, around three in the morning, they were all fast friends.

The army officers were fascinated by the tales Mohr and Kesselheim told of the convoy battles, and the two U-boat men soon had their bedazzled audience convinced that even Dönitz had to consult them in order to run the U-boat war!

When they left the night club, they all went home with one of the officers who lived nearby and continued the party until Mohr and Kesselheim had to leave. They picked up their gear at the hotel, and having delayed almost too long, had to break into a dead run to catch their train.

They fell panting and disheveled into a compartment already occupied by a French priest, who greeted them politely. He asked their destination, and taking pity on their bedraggled condition, told them they could go to sleep if they wanted to . . . He would wake them when they arrived. They accepted gratefully and were asleep in seconds.

The priest waked them shortly before they pulled

into the station at Lorient, and bade them farewell with a gentle smile and best wishes.

"Come on and go with me this trip," Mohr said impulsively when they got back to base. "I can get you a transfer."

Kesselheim was on the point of accepting, but then he said, "Let me take my leave first. I just came from a patrol on U-602, then a course at the radio school, and I haven't had any leave yet."

"All right," Mohr agreed. "But as soon as I get back from this one, I'll get you transferred back to me."

"When are they taking you off the boat?" Kesselheim asked.

"They're supposed to now, after this cruise," Mohr replied with a grin. "But I'm going to talk Uncle Karl into letting me go back."

Kesselheim nodded, thinking that Jochen Mohr could very probably talk anybody into anything he wanted. Certainly Kesselheim was ready to follow him anywhere on earth. He hesitated—but no, first his leave, then he would come back to Mohr. Next trip they would go together, and it would be like old times. They shook hands on it.

Chapter Thirteen

GERMAN U-BOAT Headquarters in Paris received a brief signal from Mohr on April 1, 1943, reporting contact with a convoy at approximately 41-02 N, 15-39 W. This first signal came at 1845, and Mohr sent two other contact reports at 1935 and 2050, respectively. Dönitz then signaled him that no other boats were in the vicinity, thus releasing him to attack.

On the evening of April 3, Dönitz signaled Mohr asking for a situation report, since he had heard nothing since he had released him to attack. There was no answer to this nor to Dönitz's request for a position report.

Tension and anxiety grew as the hours passed without further word. And as the hours lengthened into days, hope faded and U-124 was listed as missing—officially missing, but the men who waited in vain for a signal knew she was lost.

Admiral Dönitz announced her loss in a brief communiqué, and some months later, Wolfgang Frank wrote a moving tribute to "Mohr, a born convoy fighter," which appeared in the January 3, 1944, edition of the Brüsseler Zeitung.

All Germany mourned her loss. But especially affected were the men who had known the boat and her lost crew so intimately. Some of the old crew, Kesselheim particularly, were haunted by the feeling that they should have been aboard. Mohr's words, "Come with me this trip," rang in his ears. He had been so close to accepting. Perhaps he could have done something to save her. More than one of these former U-124 men has tormented himself with endless questions. "Was it *my* replacement, perhaps inexperienced, that made the fatal mistake?"

In the light of British accounts, it is more probable that her loss was due to the fact that the British escorts in this convoy carried radar. Long before BLACK SWAN could have been seen from the U-boat's bridge, she had located U-124 and was coming in to attack.

Weeks after the battle, Commander Thomson and Captain Smythe were informed that their joint attack in the pre-dawn hours of April 2, 1943, had destroyed a U-boat. They were told it was the U-124, but the war had been over for 17 years before they learned her commander's name.

Today, Commander Thomson (now Thomson-Moore) is retired and lives at his family estate in Ireland. Captain Smythe, retired from the Navy, is still at sea, master of the Union Castle Liner, RMS PENDENNIS CASTLE. He regularly passes near the scene of this old battle as he sails between England and South Africa.

When U-124 went to her grave in the Atlantic off Oporto, she carried Jochen Mohr and all her crew with her. Others, who had served aboard for one or more cruises, found a sailor's grave on some other boat—but some were lucky enough to survive the war. With only 7,000 survivors from a total strength of 39,000, the German U-boat arm had suffered the worst defeat of any branch of service in any war in history.

Karl Rode now lives in Bremen, and he and his wife and son are still invariably drawn to the sea for vacations. Karl Kesselheim and his family live in Koblenz; Rolf Brinker, his wife, two daughters and a son, live in Wuppertal-Cronenberg in the heart of the Ruhr. Egon Subklew is a *Fregattenkapitän* in the German Navy, now attached to NATO in Norway. Dr. Hubertus Goder, a practicing physician, lives with his family in Gniessau i. Holstein.

Wilhelm Schulz, a successful businessman in Hamburg, where he lives with his wife and two daughters, finished his career as a naval officer as commander of a U-flotilla on the Baltic. There, in the black days of the capitulation, he would disobey the last order given to him by Dönitz, whom he had followed so long and so faithfully.

While the Navy waited for the code word, "Regenbogen" (Rainbow), which was the order to scuttle all warships, it was rescinded by Dönitz, who was buying time with the only currency he possessed, German warships, including his own beloved U-boats. The short time thus purchased would allow many thousands more soldiers and refugees to reach western Germany, in addition to the more than two million people that had been transported through the Baltic to the west in the last three months of the war.

When Dönitz's order went out to turn over all warships intact to the Allies, some U-boat commanders, not believing the Big Lion was actually willing to surrender the ships, took matters into their own hands and scuttled their boats, despite orders.

Schulz, determined that neither his boats, materiel, men, nor himself would fall into Russian hands, blew up all boats, supplies, fuel, and ammunition. Then he loaded his men and food stores onto his one remaining vessel, a small transport, and sailed to the island of Fehmarn, near Kiel in the Baltic sea.

With him he brought a precisely detailed document accounting for every single item that had been in his possession as flotilla commander, and what disposition he had made of it. This was for the benefit of whatever authority, German or Allied, he would be called on to answer to. He left nothing for the Russians as he brought his men back to the west, and with the papers in his hand, he was prepared to face whatever consequences awaited him.

Grossadmiral Karl Dönitz, Commander in Chief of the Kriegsmarine, was named Hitler's successor when the Führer killed himself in the devastation of Berlin. And so on him fell the mantle of leadership at the time of total collapse—when there was nothing left to lead. This post he held for twenty days as he worked to bring some sort of order out of the chaos of Germany, and to see that as few as possible of his countrymen were captured by the Russians.

After the war, he was tried at Nuremburg. Both he and his U-boat branch were unequivocally cleared of the accusations of war crimes. One instance only of a U-boat firing on survivors was proved, and in this one the commander insisted that he did not know there were survivors among the wreckage which he sank to conceal his own presence. He was hanged.

Dönitz served a ten-year sentence at Spandau Prison. Cleared of the charges of war crimes leveled at himself and the U-boat branch, he was convicted of having, in peacetime, trained his men to fight and having them ready to do so when war was declared.

His wife died in 1962, and Dönitz now lives alone in Aumühle, near Hamburg.

This was U-124, the U-boat that was the edelweiss, and these were some of the men who knew her and made her great. She was the third most successful submarine, all nations included, of World War II. During her brief life, she sank one cruiser, one corvette, and 47 merchant ships with a total of 226,946 gross register tons.

ANNOUNCING AN EXCITING NEW SERIES . . .

BALLANTINE'S ILLUSTRATED HISTORY OF WORLD WAR II

From the publisher of the most complete and authentic war books in paperback—an entirely new series of BIG-SIZE original war histories, fully illustrated with about 150 photographs, maps, and accurate scale drawings of German, Japanese, British, and American weapons: battleships, submarines, and aircraft carriers; tanks and self-propelled artillery; fighter planes, medium and heavy bombers; machine guns, mines, and small arms.

Each book contains 160 pages and measures 8¼" by 5½"—**50% larger than the book you are reading**—and each is the accurate, impartial, factual account of a famous combat service, battle, or campaign as described by experienced combat leaders and eminent military historians. Sir Basil Liddell Hart, world-famous military authority, has been engaged in an advisory capacity as special Military Consultant for the entire series. The Editor is Barrie Pitt, himself the author of many military histories and chief historical advisor to the BBC television series "The Great War." The illustrations and photographs for the entire series are prepared with the cooperation and counsel of the Imperial War Museum, London.

[see next page]

... FOR COLLECTORS AND MILITARY HISTORIANS.

"A unique and exciting publishing venture . . . exceptionally well illustrated."

—**Boston Globe**

"An auspicious start . . . Emphasis is on photographs, some of rare vintage, yet the text in each case is solid and authoritative, written with spirit. Readers will find these books a bargain, not only because of their price but also their contents."

—Martin Blumenson, former Chief Historian U.S. Office of Military History, writing in the **Washington Sunday Star**

Published in groups of 4 in January, May and September. *Now available:*

GROUP 1

AFRIKA KORPS, by Major K. J. Macksey

THEIR FINEST HOUR: The Story of the Battle of Britain 1940, by Edward Bishop

D-DAY: Spearhead of Invasion, by R. W. Thompson

U-BOAT: The Secret Menace, by David Mason

GROUP 2

STALINGRAD: The Turning Point, by Geoffrey Jukes

AIRCRAFT CARRIER: The Majestic Weapon, by Donald Macintyre

PANZER DIVISION: The Mailed Fist, by Major K. J. Macksey, M.C.

BASTOGNE: The Road Block, by Peter Elstob

GROUP 3*

THE SIEGE OF LENINGRAD, by Alan Wykes

THE RAIDERS: Desert Strike Force, by Arthur Swinson

ME-109, by Martin Caidin

BATTLE FOR BERLIN: Gotterdammerung, by Earl Ziemke

*Ready in September, 1969

Each book is priced at $1.00—or you can order any four books, delivered postage free to your home by sending $4.00 to

Ballantine Books, 36 W. 20th St., New York, N. Y. 10003

"Without question, one of the finest
books on World War II ever published."
—*Los Angeles Times*

THE UNITED STATES NAVY
IN WORLD WAR II

*The One Volume History, from Pearl Harbor to
Tokyo Bay—by Men Who Fought in the Atlantic
and the Pacific and by Distinguished Naval Experts,
Authors and Newspapermen*

Compiled and Edited by S. E. SMITH

*With an Introduction by Rear Admiral E. M. Eller
Director of Naval History*

1152 pages   Maps, Index   64 pages of photos
NOW IN BALLANTINE BOOKS $1.65